Are You in or Are You Out?

by Tanya Kosh

Inclusivity and exclusivity of table manners.

A light-hearted journey into a rather serious matter.

All generalisations are false, including this one.

Mark Twain

To Peter, who wants to lick his knife in front of me every time I mention table manners.

Table of Contents

ALEX KOSH

ALEX KOSH

Acknowledgements

I am extremely grateful to Phyllis, my fairy godmother, who introduced me to a couple of things that later became very important in my life. Among others, this includes playing the Benton Fletcher collection at Fenton House in Hampstead, fine dining, and champagne tastings in London. Despite being busy travelling the world with charity and educational work, not only did she manage to read the first version of this book till the very end, but she was always there for me with advice and support, professional and personal.

My heart goes to John Sweeney, my former boss, whom I offended millions of times. Despite all my regrettable misbehaviours John remained very supportive to all my endeavours if he considered them safe for humanity. My last offence was seriously gruesome. I invited John for dinner. It was a lovely restaurant not far from St. Pancras carefully chosen by John. At the very end of the enjoyable dinner, for whatever reason, I told John that we should share the bill. Don't ask me why; I really can't explain this even to myself. The bill was more than decent, and it was my invitation, and the dinner was great. Proper gentleman that he is, he didn't even blink. This book would never see daylight if he ever shared his experience with HR.

Special thanks to Alex Kosh for his wonderful illustrations to this book. I couldn't use all of them here, but you will find them on www.alexkosh.com. You can even buy the originals on www.howtoeat.net. Many thanks to Ulyana, my first guinea pig reader. The book would have been even more boring than it is if it were not for her.

And finally, thank you to Peter, who supported me the whole way through and tolerated all my faux-pas at the table and beyond more than once.

Introduction

The title of this book has nothing to do, at least directly, with Brexit. Brexit is much more serious matter than whether your fork is a shovel or not. Still, the table manners were invented by humanity to keep the different tribes peacefully at one table—at least during the times of important decisions to be made. According to one of the classics, "Dinner is served" written by Arthur Inch and Arlene Hirst, "During the Napoleonic era, the foreign minister Charles de Talleyrand firmly believed that delicious meals presented at a graciously set table were unparalleled as a diplomatic tool" (Dinner is served. A Butler's Guide to the art of the Table., 2003, S. 18)

The title for this book came to my mind in early 1990s during a dinner in London, not far from Green Park. This could have been undoubtedly my best dinner of the last century if it weren't for the fork and the knife on the empty plate in front of me.

I'll tell you more about that night of cutlery terrors later, with all the embarrassing details I kept to myself for many years. But for now it would suffice to say that the neighbour's words, meant as a quick and trivial advice on how to bring a rather obvious matter to its logical conclusion, these few words eventually turned out to be a door opener into the world I somehow always knew existed over there, but could never imagine neither importance nor sheer depth and width of it. The world of table manners. And table mementoes. Some to remember, some to forget.

This is how I found myself on a road leading to fascinating discoveries, mind-broadening learnings and many more questions than answers. On a journey of exciting observations, interesting meetings, enthralling conversations, witnessing the

ALEX KOSH

subtleties of sophistication of human conventions, but also profound abuse bordering with bullying and humiliation. Psychology, sociology, market research – all the things I learned at the universities and practised for living came in very handy. Working for many years for multinational companies with subsidiaries and business partners all over the world helped me see the mind-boggling reality of variations of something that seemed so simple when my granny kept nagging me "Take your elbows off the table, darling." And "sit straight, Tanya."

There are plenty of manuals on table manners out there and this book is not one of them. This is rather an attempt to look behind the manuals, to understand the intrinsic connections between our psychological and other needs and the role table manners play in our lives.

I am far away from any attempt to present these notes, clearly biased and gravitating to my own experience, as academic research. It is not and is not meant to be. I see it more like an exercise aimed at marking important aspects to be investigated further, pencilling the initial frame for extra analysis. It is an attempt to look at table manners as an important cultural mechanism, instrumental for satisfaction of core human needs at all levels, from basic physiology to need for growth and personal and social development and achievements. This might also help the pupils of table manners in their learnings, as it is always easier to remember "what" if you have some idea "why."

While there is not much scientific rigor in this book, I have used a method of observation long praised by anthropologists, ethnographers and market researchers—. In reality it meant people-watching, eavesdropping, and trying to make some sense out of it all. I conducted interviews, in-depth and rather superficial ones, some structured, some totally inconsequential. I over-heard some rather interesting conversations and sound-bites, content-analysed social media (means enjoyed reading the posts on Facebook) and websites, read newspapers, including tabloids. As we all know, they sell, so must be representative of human interests, opinions and informational needs. ("They both read that newspaper. "I know it's rubbish," Sylvia giggles, "but it's wonderful rubbish, isn't it?") (York, 2007). I read magazines and books of different sorts and genres. Snobbery could be a driving force for progress. But researcher cannot afford the luxury of being selective. It is called biased sample and is frown upon by the gurus of the industry.

And, of course, I looked at my own experience. Sometimes with eyes wide shut. Hence the book has some rather sad (from my point of view) side-line stories, which you will find in this book under the common title "Table Mementoes" in-between more serious chapters. All of them unfortunately true. The only consolation is that it might be useful to etiquette teachers in search of real life hideous examples and will help the reader to understand how I arrived at some conclusions I made in this book.

I could have called this book, at least those spin-off stories "A little book of gigantic table horrors. How to stop them coming to you." But I don't know how. I think they like being written about so insist on visiting me from time to time. I am not ready yet to tell you what came to the dinner yesterday.

"An outlander's guide to the minefield of peaceful dining" was dismissed when I realised that singing "Thank you for the fish" (Adams, 1997) doesn't work every time as a polite exit line.

May be, for a sequel: "More horrors around the table. My second helping. "

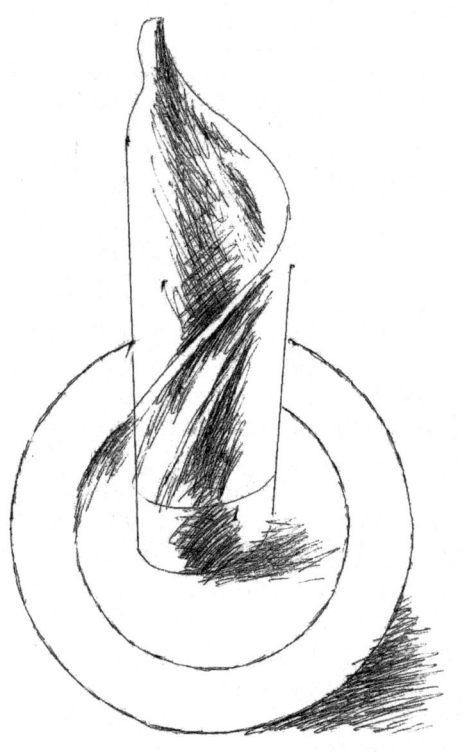

For the sake of sequel and to satisfy my own basic need to write another book, I came up with the convincing idea that all the thoughts in this book are in dire need of quantification. I like putting percentages next to the statement. Makes me look clever. So the website www.howtoeat.net has been setup recently with the aim to get as many responses as possible from people from different walks of life, different backgrounds, different cultures, and different countries.

Whether you read this book till the very end or not, go to www.howtoeat.net and let me know what you think by answering our questions. Pass the link to the questionnaire, please, to all of your friends, who are not averse to the topic of table manners. There are no right or wrong answers. As there are no universally good manners, appropriate in any circumstances as you will find out reading this book. If you are "in" somewhere, you are "out" somewhere else. And the other way round. It's only as good as it makes you feel.

Chapter 1. A few words about cultural competence.

You can often hear that someone has manners. And someone doesn't. You might have even said it yourself. In fact, it is not true. Everyone has manners. The question is what sort of manners those are. Good or bad, someone would say. But what is good and what is bad is a matter of convention, a matter of social concord, and individual taste.

The last two decades in the field, as researchers call their empirical exercises, taught me one main thing—there is no such a thing as universally good or universally bad manners. Every plant could be a weed if out of place.

There is possibly only one universally bad table manner – bringing danger to the table, but there are so many ways of doing it. Even not washing your hands before eating could be a good habit in some circumstances.

And I am not talking about jungles or slums. Just a recent warning in March 2016 when thousands of people in Derbyshire and Leicestershire, England, were warned not to use tap water for any purpose because of incredibly high levels of chlorine detected (BBC News, 2016).

Certain normally good manners could be bad and damaging both to an individual and to a social group if practised in a wrong place at a wrong time.

Wrong circumstances could make the best manners at best eccentric, at worst – dangerous. Just try to imagine yourself in a black tie dress at pre-Arsenal football match do in a Holloway road pub, buying a bottle of port and insisting on the bottle going clockwise (Wallop, 2009) only when the

ALEX KOSH

punter to your right has an empty glass. And no, it is not considered a good manner to say hello to people you don't know on the streets of London. But it is an absolute must when you hike in the Alps.

Cultural competence is the term coined and used mainly for analysing and understanding the differences between different nations, races and ethnic groups. The concept is widely used in healthcare in the US. Wikipedia gives the narrow definition of the term: "Cultural competence can be defined as the level of knowledge-based skills required to provide effective clinical care to patients from a particular ethnic or racial group." (Wikipedia, 2016)

In business, the term cultural (or often cross-cultural) competence is used when it comes to multinational business environment. Articles like "How to give feedback to different nationalities?," "Do you understand your boss in another country?" or "How to make you virtual team work despite the time and cultural differences?" are plenty.

Table manners constitute an important part of cultural competence whether you travel on business or for pleasure. Or host people from other countries in your hometown. A trifle, like how you like your beer served can leave you out, preventing you from joining in and enjoying the fun.

Say you are English and go to Oktoberfest in Munich. You like beer; it is your drink of choice. You anticipate your first mass (beer mug 1, holds 1 litre). You know how you like your beer to look, how you like it to taste. And here it comes. With a beer head a third of a mug tall. That's how they do it in Germany. Beer should have a head. Even if you serve it at home.

Many English friends and colleagues of mine felt puzzled. Andrew even asked the waiter directly "and where is one-third

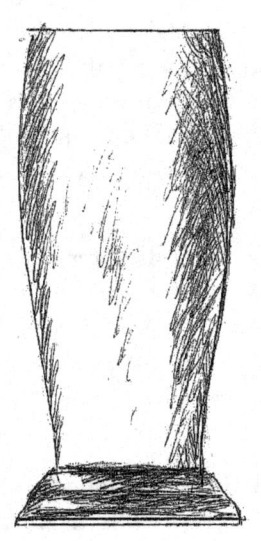

of my beer?" He felt cheated. Paid for a whole litre and got two-thirds of it.

Germans coming to England and getting their pints full, clean and clear are known for asking publicans not "to kill the best there."[1]

A colleague of mine, Karsten, sporting a rather depressed face after his first pint served "according to the local" standards at Highgate pub, which he insisted was frequented by Karl Marx, went as far as getting beyond the bar and grabbing the bartender's hand in order to ensure he gets his beer the way he likes it. Karl Marx, still in Highgate, just a few hundred meters away down the hill, surely approved. [2] The bartender wasn't amused.

According to Euromonitor International data, reported by Telegraph.co.uk (Akkoc, 2014), Germany consumes an estimated 110 litres of beer per person totalling nearly 9bn litres per year in total. UK – only half of the total amount, 4.3bn litres, which translates into 67 litres per capita. Maybe beer with the head really knows better when it comes to sales?

Differences in how you serve alcohol are not limited to beer only. The British "large glass" of wine doesn't exist in Austria. Serve it and you would be considered a low class alcoholic. You can order a "viertel" (quarter, the same 250 ml<) but it will be served in the jug and the waiter will pour only something like 125 or even less in your glass.

Cultural competence isn't limited only to interactions between different nationalities.

You would come across different cultural groups within the most homogeneous society. You can call them classes or socio-demographic groups.

A wider and better explanation of what cultural competence

is about is given by SAMHSA: "Cultural competence is the ability to interact effectively with people of different cultures. In practice, both individuals and organizations can be culturally competent. 'Culture' is a term that goes beyond race or ethnicity. It can also refer to such characteristics as age, gender, sexual orientation, disability, religion, income level, education, geographical location, or profession." (SAMHSA, 2016)

Each social group irrespective of its size develops its own specific culture over time. Among the most obvious signs that help us to differentiate between cultures are jargons and/or dialects, rituals, habits, dress codes, and manners.

In social discourse, cultural competence is not the knowledge of literature, art, or philosophy. It is rather an ability to identify, understand and manage the differences between you own culture and the cultures you deal with. The ability to adapt to those differences.

As a result, cultural competence is an ability to communicate and cooperate efficiently with the representatives of cultures different to your own, be it demographic cohorts, social classes or social and professional groups. Say, me trying to convince teenagers using my drive as a skate park to move somewhere else. Never ever managed this one.

The individual need for cultural competence appears only when the person leaves their comfort zone and familiar surroundings, when he or she is forced to interact with social groups previously unfamiliar or totally unknown. It is higher in countries with diverse population and thriving social mobility.

I interviewed a former colleague of mine from the German-speaking part of Switzerland whose only move in life was from one side of the lake to another one. He was already 30 when he joined an international organisation. He remembers very well the first time he realised he needed to do something to become more efficient in his work. He had to learn German.

Schweitzer Deutsch (Swiss German) is rather different to Hoch Deutsch, which is a standardised form of German language used in formal and written communication and for communication between Germans speaking different dialects. Something similar to BBC English.

Swiss German was absolutely enough for leisure travels of which he did quite a lot. At the end of the day it is only a matter of few hours driving to reach other German-speaking countries in Europe. But soon, his language skills put him in an inferior position. *"I went back to school to learn my mother tongue,"* he says.

I was in a rather similar position during my first working year in London. I had a couple of colleagues in the department who fully understood me when my goals were beneficial to theirs, but used my accent as an excuse when the things to be done were not easy and demanded more effort to be put in.

Whether this communication happens within your own natural habitat or while interacting cross-culturally or internationally – it doesn't matter. We all want to be culturally competent when meeting other people, whether we know and use this term or not. It is a normal human longing to reach his or her goals efficiently, simplifying task solving and optimising all the dealings on the way there. Plus, they say, we look and feel smarter and better when we think we are competent. And we feel "we are in" when we reach our goals. Whether it is true or not is another matter.

Nobody likes feeling out of place. That's exactly what the lack of cultural competence when it comes to British table manners did to me on that night of cutlery terrors.

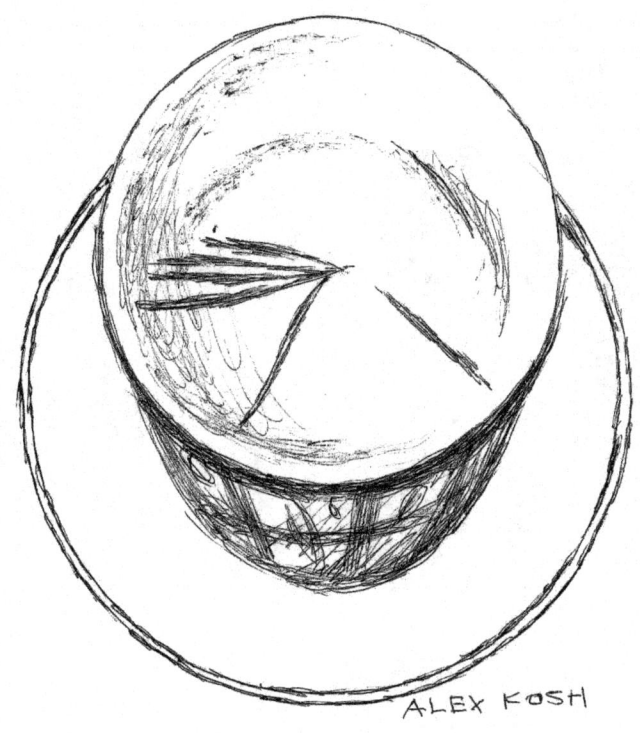

ALEX KOSH

15

Table Mementoes. The night of cutlery terrors.

I was born and bred in Kiev, Ukraine when it was still part of the Soviet Union. In addition to all the "science set" (algebra, geometry, physics, chemistry, biology, distorted history etc.), we also had some housekeeping lessons. Table manners were part of the curriculum. They taught us how to hold your knife and fork, all about the table linen, which crockery to use for whatever food you manage to get to your table in times of deficit. As you can rightly guess, we didn't learn how to cook and eat artichokes, sushi and sashimi, lobsters, and oysters and other bourgeois obscenities. At least not in school.

During one of the interviews, I was told that the communist attempts to create a stronger feel of "us" and "others, the enemies," were not confined only to political propaganda and heavily censored media and history, rewritten beyond recognition. That "anti-bourgeoisie" mind-set penetrated other areas of life, such as the realm of etiquette and table manners in particular. To do things a little bit different, to make sure that one can spot "an enemy" at the table immediately. Or, most probably, as I don't like conspiracy theories much and the reality is always much simpler, the etiquette guidelines were compiled by those who didn't know any better and never travelled beyond the iron curtain. This is my only rational explanation to a couple of table manners I picked up as a child and had to change later.

Fast forward, I started my own market research agency in Ukraine, a country with over 55mln population at that time. Our first clients were multinationals, so I was lucky enough to have to travel on business, which I happily did.

Here I am, in London, presenting the results to the client. And, oh, how lucky, the big bosses of a market research multinational invite me to dinner to discuss the possibility of my humble company in the country (in)famous then for Chernobyl only to join them. I guess I don't have to dwell onhow I felt, what it meant for me, for my colleagues and for the whole emerging market research industry back in Ukraine. Elated would be a word too weak.

The restaurant they invited me to was not far from the Green Park Tube station in London, upmarket if not a little bit pompous, sort of an old-school type, or so it seemed to me. Very much suitable for the company (except me). My hosts were professional and at the same time very nice, charming human beings. The service was impeccable; I hardly noticed it till the moment when we finished our starters and everyone put the knives and the forks back on the empty plate. So did I. Exactly the way we were taught at school and practised ever after.

I like the break between the starter and the main course. The anticipation of more delicious food (and wine), everyone still being hungry enough to enjoy what is coming next, but not too hungry to be unable to think about other things rather than food. Relaxed enough to engage in a pleasant exchange of thoughts, experiences, ideas and opinions. Unless the break starts feeling a little bit too long, for no apparent reason whatsoever.

A senior partner makes an old corny joke about the chef going fishing first, otherwise why would they call it "a catch of the day." The empty starter plates are still in front of us. The waiter is nearby hovering noticeably.

I look at the plates and get an insight – all plates are empty, and I just have a lone salad left sitting in the middle of mine. I think I understand my mistake, pick up my cutlery (or should I call it silver? It actually was). And with a smug feeling – Hey, I solved the problem! – I finish my food. Yes, they did tell us at school that it is not only impolite to start eating before everyone has his or her food served, but it is also impolite to clean the table when someone is still eating. Aren't I clever? I put the cutlery back.

Apparently not. Although my attempts are noticed. I get a strange look from the waiter. Something in between curiosity and disbelief. I'll think about it tomorrow, I tell myself. I do practise self-analysis combined with the situational one sometimes. But at the moment I expect some instant gratification for my forward thinking. At least some action on the waiter's side.

Nothing happens. He still hangs out somewhere at a distance and looks frozen. That's how the talk around the table starts feeling too. But the conversation picks up, or to be correct, the senior boss on my left indulges into a monologue about the importance of aiming at representative sample in polling, and the lady in front of me is too busy waiting for a break to add her own essential thoughts to this vital subject.

That's when the handsome young man on my right gets closer. Would have been not too bad on any other night out. But not today – I am too busy negotiating my deal. And the service in this place is rather annoying. My neighbour whispers: "Put it on twelve." What sort of a code is this? The man realises that my English is obviously in dire need of enhancement and re-phrases his whisper: "The knife. And the fork. Put it in the middle of the plate. The waiter thinks you are still eating, although he cannot figure it out."

My cutlery is perfectly positioned across my plate. I never failed my Ukrainian etiquette teachers in my life before. But I

ALEX KOSH

have a nagging feeling I won't follow their instructions in future either. Knife's handle is on the right. Fork's on the left. The knife and the fork cross each other, exactly in the middle of the plate, so the tines are on the right, with blade over the fork, pointing to the left. What's the problem? The very next nanosecond I notice how well-behaved the other people's silver is. Pointing at twelve hours, knife and fork lie parallel to each other, placed at bottom-centre, knife's blade turned inside. Observational research never ever made more sense in my life.

My hands start shaking. I commit another crime at the table (even I know it is a crime) – producing some creepy noise, hitting in a process of re-adjustment everything I can. The knife hits the plate, the fork hits the knife. I am so happy that the representative sample is such an important topic that they don't notice at all my mishaps. Otherwise, I imagine with trepidation, they would all look at me, tut-tutting and rolling their eyes. No, they never would, but this I understand a bit later.

The plates miraculously disappear and the main course comes.

By the end of the evening the business agreement is reached. I guess the deal we were discussing was never under any direct threat. But who knows.

Chapter 2. A tiny bit of history and theory

Without understanding some theory and history behind, the table manners realm might seem to some "a mile wide and an inch deep." But this is not the case.

The word "Etiquette" is tightly connected to "high society" first of all simply due to its linguistic routes, the fact very well-known and very well described in an enjoyable to read and informative manner by John Daly (Daly, 2014)

"It shouldn't surprise you that the French started it all! Today's etiquette began in the French royal courts in the 1600s and 1700s. Etiquette used to mean "keep off the grass." When Louis XIV's gardener at Versailles discovered that the aristocrats were trampling through his garden, he put up signs, or "etiquettes," to warn them off, but the dukes and duchesses walked right past the signs. Finally, the king himself had to decree that no one was to go beyond the bounds of the etiquettes."

John is very quick to correct himself that the rules of etiquette itself existed well before "French," providing the fascinating facts about the numerous earlier "etiquette" books, going as far back as Egyptian society in 2400 BC. But still keeps the connection between etiquette and upper classes.

This is in some way correct, as the very discussion of good manners would be more often happening between those involved in organising and managing if not ruling the social interactions rather than between those whose livelihood depended on long hours of manual labour. Still one shouldn't assume that the latter were without their own "etiquettes." They just called them differently.

* Terminology

Kate Fox, in her enthralling book, one of my favourites since I moved to London at the end of the last century, "Watching the English" (Fox, Watching the English, 2004) gets much closer to grasping the omnipresence of etiquette. She uses the term "rules" though, talking about the whole canvas of life of English, from rules of sex and rules of pub talk to rules of religion.

In fact, the word etiquette in daily life of any human in any country on this planet is not used very often. Due to linguistic origins the word is associated with upper classes. It doesn't mean that the good/appropriate manners themselves are not there or are not enforced by anyone else rather than the top 2-10% of the population. You can't take them away, whatever human interaction you are looking at. How about good table manners practised by cannibals? You might not consider them good, but they do exist, claims Margaret Visser (Visser, 1992). In her highly commended book, she talks in-depth about rituals of dinner and brilliantly covers the whole history of etiquette around dinner table.

Neither etiquette nor ritual nor even rules are the words commonly used in daily conversations. Nobody would tell you about the "ritual of washing hands" (unless it is compulsive-obsessive) or the rules of "stuffing yourself" with bangers-and-mash every Saturday. You are bound to hear much more often some of the synonyms. Those would be expressions similar to "that's what we do," or "we don't do that here." "That's not a done thing." "How appropriate." As a foreigner, you are bound to hear it much more often. Simply because you ask, if you are at least a little bit curious and willing to learn something new hoping to make yourself more culturally competent and get that tiny bit closer to be allowed to get "in."

* Etiquette. The primary purpose of etiquette and definition

There are many cultural, historical, and even biological reasons behind why it is as it is, why "that's the way it's done." Why certain habits are deeply rooted and one cannot ditch them without an effort, and in some cases, like hand-washing, better shouldn't even try to get rid of them, and why certain things are frowned upon or even strictly prohibited. Not by law or religion, but by an inner voice, helpfully whispering to you: "it's not a done thing. Stop it."

Certain etiquette teaching is doing a serious disservice to the cause when focusing on memorising apparently superficial rules, without explaining the historic and modern social reasoning behind those. It is much easier to remember and practise "whats" if you understand "whys" behind.

The etiquette is very often defined as glue which keeps society together and historically – to keep it members alive and well. It is not stale and carved in stone. It wouldn't serve its primary purpose, enabling smooth interactions and keeping people happy enough to continue functioning productively if it would hold the human development back. Humans would ditch it at the very first opportunity. Whether we admit it or not, we do actually get rid of whatever habits our grandfathers considered chief and foremost if those rules prevent us from successful cooperation and advancing. What is missing in many books, which have the very word "etiquette" in their titles, is the definition of the concept. Hence the word itself, whether on its own or combined with (table) manners is too often to my liking perceived as quaint or at worst even as outdated and snobbish. This is a totally wrong perception, because as mentioned above, manners and etiquette are always there. Even if you call them something different.

ALEX KOSH

Established etiquette is necessary to enable successful interaction within and between any social, political, or economic groups, be it a poker club or diplomatic circles. The set of rules would differ from grouping to grouping. What is a "done thing" in one country is not necessarily an acceptable practice in another. Think about wine or beer served, as described early. Think about small talk – absolutely essential component in Britain, but considered waste of time by many pragmatic Germans.

The importance of rules could vary in its degree, but the primary purpose remains as it was all those hundreds of thousands of years ago, when our ancestors first understood that no man is an island, that surviving together is easier than on your own, even if they didn't call the rules they had neither etiquette, nor good manners. "Survival guide" was possibly not in use either, but that's what it was and that's what it still is now, even if today's survival in western world tends to resemble more of "pleasant living" rather than mere physiological endurance or durability from our ancestors' point of view.

"To make enemies by unnecessary and wilful incivility is just as insane a proceeding as to set your house on fire." Arthur Schopenhauer.

* Etiquette. The main principle

Etiquette in modern western life is based on a deeply engrained concept of respect—respect to other people, to yourself, to the business employing you, and to the society you live in. When you get outside your usual circumstances, let's say, while traveling, you practise respect to the unknown, respect to yourself, to people you don't know yet, and to situations you find yourself in, till you find reasons to respect what you learn or till proven that it's not worth any veneration.

When it comes to people and social entities we simply put up with, this is not necessarily the sort of respect synonymous with admiration. This is more the sort of respect that is closer to presumption of innocence and the right of others to be treated according to law and other social rules. It goes hand in hand with the right to free speech. Etiquette rules are there to enable this right to its full potential prescribing how, when, and where to exercise it to ensure it is beneficial to the society and all the parties involved. You might disagree with some aspects of rules, behaviours, practices, or laws. You can vocalise your disagreement or take it further to some type of action, but some sort of universal respect on all levels, from individual to constitutional, is always there in a democratic society; otherwise, it cannot function.

It could be in a form of re-directed respect. When choosing to behave in a civilised way in a situation you are not comfortable in, you might not necessarily respect the receiver of your actions—the person who creates the problem for you and others. But you respect yourself, the values and norms of your culture, and people around you.

I was once at a ball where the heir to the throne of one of the countries, where monarchy was abolished at the beginning of

the last century, was present; his wife was asked a rather impertinently worded question: "How does it feel to be an heir to the throne which hasn't existed for the last hundred years?" She ignored the question, continuing the conversation for a few seconds on a topic discussed previously. Then a man appeared and took her away from the unpleasant situation.

The man was clearly there watching for signs agreed upon in advance, whether it was her touching her arm or something else, a gesture inconspicuous for onlookers, but urgent. It was dealt with respect to herself and with respect to the cause – the charity ball. The person who asked the question was left disappointed. A juicy scandal died unborn. But he wasn't able to say he was disrespected. His question was though.

Maybe the word *respect* is not the most exact in this context, as it meaning involves an instant connotation to high opinion of something, but for the lack of a better one, I will continue using it.

Cultural competence is about respect, and table manners inevitably are too. Paul Meshanko in his book "The Respect Effect: Using the Science of Neuroleadership to Inspire a More Loyal and Productive Workplace" (Meshanko, 2013) singles out the twelve rules of respect. The first one urges reader to pay special attention to non-verbal cues. Possibly, more people would stop salting and peppering their food before even trying it if explained that this is a very rude behaviour, a very strong verbal cue of total disrespect not only to the cook, but also to their own palate.

There are plenty of media features on etiquette starting with "There isn't enough respect to X Y Z today." It is a famous old adage you would find to a certain extent in any generation when people start noticing that police and doctors look a bit like children. Etiquette is changing together with the society, as good manners are there to keep society progressing, not to hold it back.

"The children now love luxury. They have bad manners, contempt for authority; they show disrespect for elders and love chatter in place of exercise." (Socrates, 2016) .

Nothing has changed, I have to admit—just the means for chatting. More and more people believe today that there is a place for mobile phones on the dining table, at least in certain business circumstances if you want to stay "in." Fully 89% of mobile phone owners say they used their phone during the most recent social gathering they attended (Zickuhr, 2015).

I believe that mobile phones are here to stay. I also believe that your work mobile has a right to be switched on (okay, on vibration) during your working hours and should be checked on a regular basis. This is with all my due respect to those who tend to see change more like a threat than a challenge and who prefer to use their experience to preserve status quo rather than to embrace the inevitable transformation.

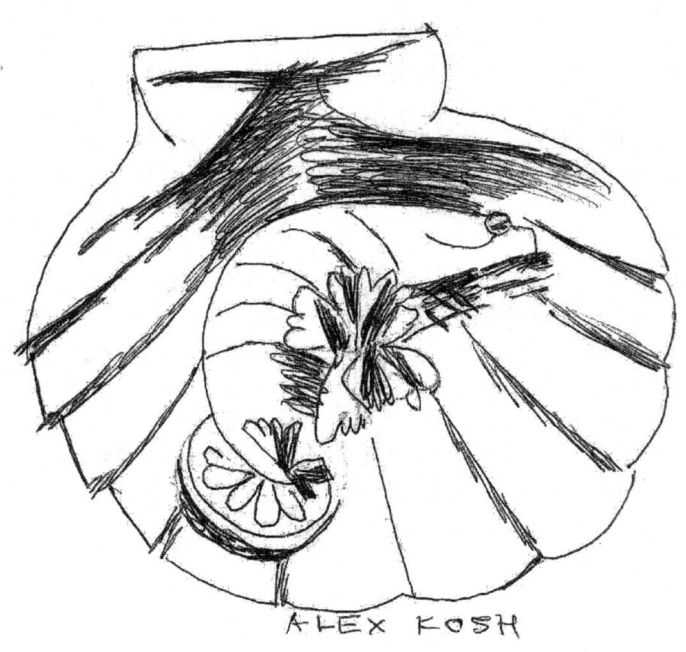

ALEX KOSH

Table mementoes. She is out to lunch.

It is a blessing to have a colleague who picks up the phone and instead of "hello" says the full introduction line with a cheerful "what can we do for you today?" at the end. She never asks our IT man mending a frozen computer whether he tried to switch it on to see if it works and never giggles with others when she has to listen to someone else indulging in sometimes-not-so-friendly banter. She doesn't bring home to work. No sandwiches with garlic to eat at the desk either. And if she is going to make a cup of tea for herself, she will definitely ask everyone around if they want some. She is a treasure, everyone says. All the files are in order, in the right folders.

It is assessment time; she passes it with flying colours. After all the formalities are completed I take her out for lunch to discuss soft topics, like how she sees her further professional growth, and then I am off to the airport. I have a project meeting on the continent in the morning. My vis-a-vis is the one to be trusted with booking the best flights for our travels and to keep our diaries in order. No one ever complained.

Being seated by the window with a perfect view over the river, we indulge in small talk about the tides in the Thames and specifically the one in London Bridge area. Some people come by boats to the office. They have boat shelters instead of garages at home. I tell her about my American friend who lives next to the Thames, saying that the stairs leading to the water are often flooded. So he keeps his office shoes in the boat and wellingtons in what he calls his "mudroom."

She is very polite; she doesn't correct my English. She just uses the word "steps" instead of stairs when she talks about her friend with a similar problem. He lives somewhere in Putney and believes that the only way to commute is by water.

We talk about business issues, career growth, and realisation of full potential. She talks about her ambitions, sharing with me that she wanted this conversation to be mindful and focused. And she is very pleased that it is.

My mobile rings. I apologise and pick it up from the bag. Lunch or not, work is not confined to a particular place or to strictly defined time anymore; it is a state of mind. If you work for a multinational, it is not only the new office culture enabled by new technology, it is also about the time zones and some countries working Sundays but having their offices closed on Fridays.

She smiles politely, but I can see that she is not amused. She believes that there is no place for the phone on the dining table whatsoever, business meeting or not, that mobile phones are now becoming not only an extension to the hand, but also to the head. And this is dangerous. We might be replaced by robots sooner than we think.

She doesn't say anything now, but I've heard her saying this before. She switched her own phone off this morning before our meeting and left it on her desk when we went out for lunch. Miss Manners she is. And proud of it.

Service has been a bit clumsy, and I wouldn't mind this particularly disagreeable waiter to be replaced by a clean and efficient robot. Suddenly I imagine being old and patronised by my personal AI[3] carer (Pym, 2015). It might have a similar facial expression on its screen as I see in front of me. Slightly disapproving.

It says "private number" on the display, which usually makes me wary, but I answer anyway. It is my former colleague on the phone. He moved to the client side recently. After a rather short introductory chit-chat, he asks me about my plans for the evening as someone dropped out and as a last minute replacement I could join them at their corporate do where I could meet other major players in the industry. Central London, nice location," he says.

Blimey. I don't mind being a last-minute replacement. I don't know where they hold this, but I would travel to whatever place he would mention. Doesn't have to be nice. Although I assume it is seriously nice. This is an incredible chance for me to meet all the decision makers of our top clients. It would take me years to organise the meetings to meet them. If I ever succeeded. We normally talk to "gate-keepers," junior people in the organisation who are not always in a position to make a serious decision.

And there is a bonus too. The major players include a very famous columnist, whose features I read every week. She is that very reason to buy that newspaper. She is the woman I adore and never even dreamt of meeting her in flesh. Not to mention imagining a possibility of talking to her. What a present. What an opportunity. What an impossible temptation to resist. And I say: "Bugger. I have a plane to catch."

"OK. Till next then." He disappears. I don't even have a chance to ask him for his new phone numbers. Next time then.

I ask for the bill and pay. We say goodbyes. I get into the taxi. After some ride into the direction of the airport my phone rings. It's her.

"Hi," she says. "I've just checked my mobile. You can turn back. They've cancelled your meeting this morning. I'd better cancel your flight right now. Isn't it wonderful to have a free evening to spend at home?"

Chapter 3. Classification of table manners

Whether you accept the newly emerging manners as they come or not, you could be sure that they still will serve the old purposes even if with a modern twist to it.

If you look at the whole range of table manners you notice in different cultures, you should be able to see the similarities. It is not about food only. Table manners evolved together with the development of humanity and its needs.

The table manners across the world are clearly serving three common purposes:

* mere survival of humanity in general and individuals in particular;
* amplification of enjoyment of food consumption; and
* social identification and self-esteem, and in some rather extreme cases like mine, self-actualisation.

Or shall I call it further in the book, devoting a separate chapter to each

* "Health and Safety,"
* "The table of joy" and
* "ID rules" fake and real ones?

To give some background to this suggested classification, let's talk first about the hierarchy of human needs as our table manners, as many other things in our lives are intrinsically connected to what we require as human beings. Maslow's hierarchy of needs was one of the first things I learned while doing my psychology degree.

I read many articles criticising the simplicity of the approach and other faults of the concept, but still I believe it makes perfect sense in case of table manners, especially for its simplistic and clean and clear approach. I do believe that if the idea is really meaningful, you should be able to explain it to the five-year-old without hiding behind sophisticated words and heavy academic constructions.

For illustration/reminder purposes, I would like to use the pyramid here (Wikipedia, 2016). You cannot go any further with simplification. Maslow never drew the pyramid himself. This was done by his followers, possibly trying explaining it to someone much younger.

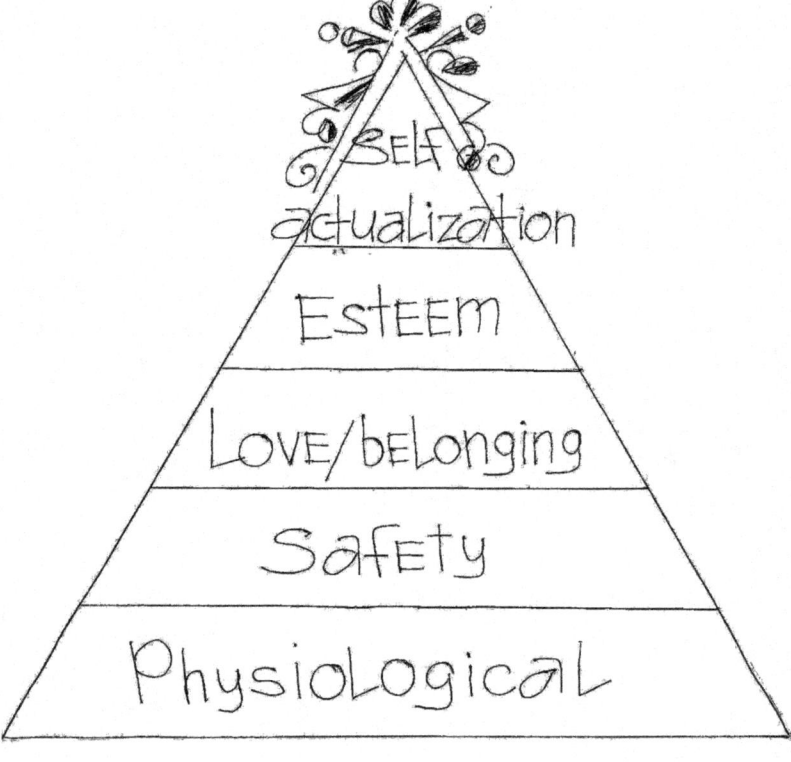

Table manners evolve around the basic human need – food, a source of energy. But they are much more important than satisfying a basic physiological need in an acceptable manner.

Attitude to food changes when the level of prosperity grows. At a basic level of physiological survival, people are happy to have any food. Be it agricultural conditions in the country, say severe drought, political and economic mismanagement or just individual financial circumstances, if you don't get enough calories daily, you wouldn't really be impressed by advice to eat organic only or to balance your diet towards super foods. Many former and current students would know what I am talking about remembering the days when we had to choose whether to buy a sandwich or a bus ticket.

When the situation improves and the basic need is securely satisfied, having more money and hence more choice, people start thinking of quality of food.

Organic food became mass market only when the average well-being levels allowed marketers to move their communication from availability and price towards quality.

At this stage you know that there is enough food for you over there and you can afford to eat every day. You have enough resource available to move up the needs' ladder. You start thinking "how safe is it? Are there any unnecessary chemicals in my food? How can I help my body to become healthier and fitter? Are the animals kept properly? Is produce sustainable and environmentally friendly?"

Of course, you have table manners at every stage. But it is only when people (and the social group/class/family they belong to) are totally sure that there is enough food of good quality guaranteed on their tables every day, sure to the extent that they never ever even think about it, not in these terms anyway, the focus around food and its consumption shifts to presentation of food, table and humans around it.

The overwhelming majority of table manners, nearly all of them serve several purposes hence belong to more than one group at the same time.

For example, the rule of not talking with your mouth full is a safety rule preventing you from choking, but it is also your personal safety of not embarrassing yourself with food getting out of your mouth or not allowing yourself to be misunderstood if your speech is not very clear. Such a behaviour also doesn't add to enjoyment of other people around the table, hence the rules of "Table of Joy" do not allow it either. It is less of an "ID" manner as basic safety manners are wide-spread across different social groups. Still it is a tell-tale sign of person's upbringing and background. Many would agree that it is not a pleasant environment to bring up children in if there are no adults around being able to say, "Don't talk with your mouth full."

Let's see how it works

Chapter 4. Health and safety

Never ever bring danger to the table.

One of the basic functions of table manners is to ensure that we survive as human species—that we eat the right food in the right quantities and neither we nor our guests fall ill. That we are not injured or killed by neighbours while eating. That our off-springs, which are much more vulnerable in their infancy than other species' babies, have a good chance to grow up. That eating doesn't translate into self-harm. Inclusivity in this group historically meant one major thing—you stay alive.

* Health

It starts with basic hygiene. If you are seriously hungry you might not care whether you have appropriate cutlery and whether your napkin (if you have one) is of the right colour, size and shape. The belly has no ears. You simply need something fit for human consumption—preferably fresh and nutritious. It's good if you have some healthy habits in place, but compulsive night-time eating disorder, when people wake up at night and eat, usually after the visit to the bathroom, hardly ever involves sophisticated table layout and linen napkins. Let's hope that the hands are washed prior to a fridge being open.

Humanity cared about hygiene long before Louis Pasteur and his tiny discoveries. Some basic table manners were developed based on experience just to make sure that people don't fall ill through transmitting microbes from contaminated surfaces to food they eat even nobody at that time would explain these rules by reference to bacteria. For example, this is one of the basic functions of cutlery. You expect it to be cleaner than your hands.

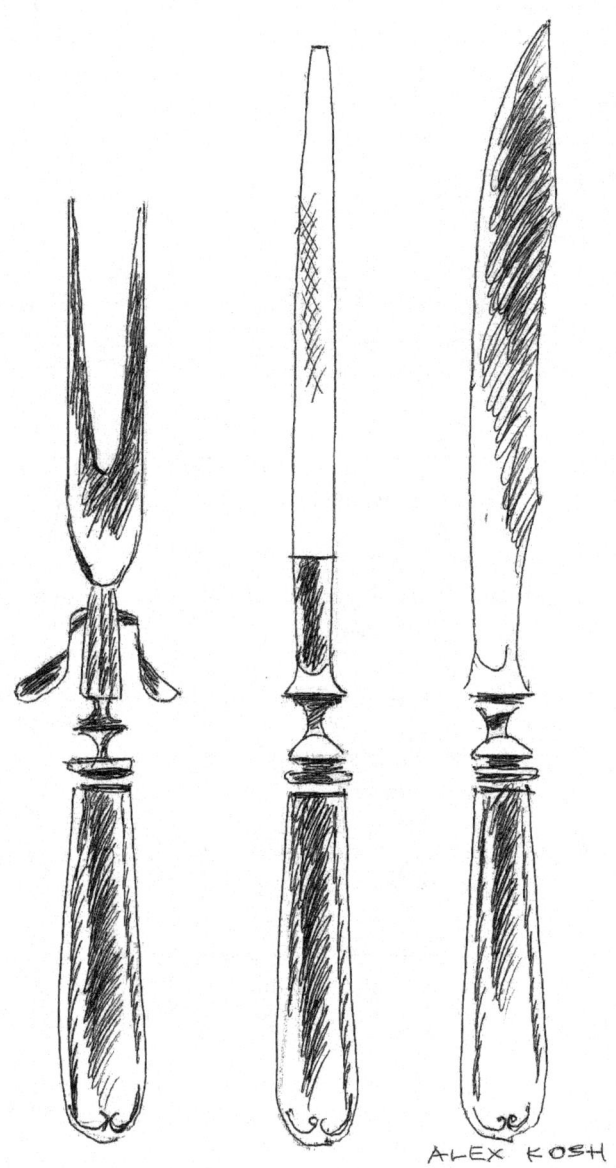

ALEX KOSH

40

This group of manners is self-evident. But please be aware that even this basic group of manners is not universal. Taking care of one's health appropriately is not a manner – it is a basic principle of life and should be applied aptly, depending on circumstances. Otherwise you are not "in" anywhere any more, but rather "out forever."

* Wash your hands before eating. But never in contaminated waters. It will do you more harm than good. It's not a Montezuma's revenge. It's your own negligence.

* Take care of your grooming before joining the table. Unkempt appearance is perceived as a threat to our health. We don't want to share our food with someone who could be full of germs. But, unfortunately, a polished look is no guarantee from any contagious nasties.

* Use clean cutlery. Normally, it is cleaner than hands. Or don't use the cutlery if this would offend your host. Just make sure that your hands are of certain hygiene standards.

* Hygiene is the reason why left hand is never used for eating in some cultures.

* Don't pick food or cutlery off the floor. Ask the waiter to replace it (or do it yourself in the majority of cases). And no, there is really no 20-seconds rule. Sorry.

* Don't use your hands to pick up food leftovers or bones from your mouth, unless you are really in danger of imminent death if you don't get that

fishbone out now. Who knows what you can spread later on touching something or someone with your hands.

* The glass you drink from should be clean. It is all right to ask for it to be replaced if it is not.

But humans wouldn't be humans if they wouldn't try to break the rules or at least to find a loophole. "Know the rules well, so you can break them effectively." (Dalai Lama XIV, 2016). And efficiency is important. What do you do if the guests are nearly there, you can hear the sound of gravel, last final touches to the perfectly set table, and then, oh horror, you see the dishwasher mark on one of the glasses?

Apparently, there are tricks of the trade for every professional challenge life throws at you. I was lucky enough to have the opportunity to talk to couple of butlers. One of them mentioned the best kept butlers' secret. When laying the table and finding the odd dirty glass, one would lick the mark and polish the glass immediately.

It has been also scientifically proven that human saliva is the best cleaner ever, even for your computer screen: "The use of human saliva to clean dirty surfaces has been an intuitive practice for many generations…Saliva has long been widely used as a cleaning agent for all kinds of surfaces and has shown good performance, especially on gold-leaf objects." (Paula M. S. Romão, Vol. 35, No. 3 (Aug., 1990)).

Effective? Yes. Hygienic? No. Some of the secrets should remain secret. Count me out on this one.

Overwhelming desire/need to stay healthy defines many rules of etiquette. And I am not talking here about not puking

ALEX KOSH

on the table or into the plate. You are not supposed to pick up food between your teeth with your finger – use the toothpick you can safely dispose of.

Americans are stricter on many health related rules. While you can use toothpicks even at the posh table in England, just cover your mouth with the other hand, I would recommend doing so somewhere private in the US. Burping at the table is no go in the majority of countries as it might signify disease which could be contagious. Still one should stay culturally competent when travelling to China. Apparently, belching is not only acceptable but might be even expected as it is seen as a sign of appreciation. (Boscamp, 2013)

Blowing your nose should be done in private. And never ever blow your nose in the paper napkin provided on the table and then put it back on the table or on the empty plate.

> *"He actually looked all right, rather nice I would say. Till he did that. And then put this dirty paper napkin on the plate for me to clean. How am I supposed to touch it? The only thing I wanted when I saw this was to pick it up with some spaghetti tongs and stick it into his white shirt's pocket. Even better if it would be already wet in the gravy from his plate,"* said one of the waiters I interviewed.

* Safety

Can you eat when you are scared? I can't. Quite a few people I interviewed know the feeling. Losing a pound or two during exams time is not that uncommon.

Most of the fears keeping us awake at night and stressed during the day are intangible. They don't have big teeth and glowing eyes; they don't make howling sounds. They also don't brandish huge swords; neither would they make any other verbal or non-verbal threats.

They are mainly in our heads and in many cases they don't seem that awful in the morning. I used to worry about the fence on the left side of my garden. Being old and half rotten, it kept falling into my garden. There were no flowers there it could have damaged. And the best thing - it was even not my responsibility; it was the neighbours' fence. Still it kept me away from sleep.

Our psychological and physiological response to intangible and even imaginary fears is still the same as it was when the only choice we had was flight or fight.

Hardly any living creature can eat when its life seems to be in danger. For example, when we are scared, our mouths dry up. Without saliva, the desire for food diminishes significantly or simply disappears.

Our bodies produce enormous amount of hormones to enable us to react adequately, provide more blood to legs and hands than to any other organs and to put it in a nutshell, to enable us to forget about anything else not crucial to escape from imminent danger. It is not only food consumption that is not possible when people perceive some threat, whether real or not. It is also digestion and food assimilation which are affected.[4]

"Dr. Herbert M. Shelton once described an experiment performed on a cat that had just finished eating. The cat's stomach was observed with X rays, and digestion was proceeding normally. A dog was then brought into the room and the cat took notice. Immediately all digestive processes in the cat halted. Its stomach ceased moving and the digestive juices stopped secreting. When the dog was removed, the cat's digestion resumed." (Raw Food Explained, 2016)

While all the research quoted is rather recent, the knowledge of this type of body response is not. For hundreds of years, etiquette of eating and partying addresses the need of safety in many ways.

Eating is aggressive by nature, and the implements required for it could quickly become weapons; table manners are, most basically, a system of taboos designed to ensure that violence remains out of the question. (Visser, 1992)

For example, why do you have to keep your knife always with its blade inside? Even when you finished eating, you should put it with blade facing to the left, inside the plate. This habit originated many years ago. Once upon a time Europe was populated by different tribes more often fighting each other than not. But the threat from barbarians and other enemies required unions. Negotiations often happened during or were followed by eating and drinking. And it does not make much sense to spend years on developing relationships with potential allies to have them killed at the agreement celebration dinner.

"Game of Thrones" is not that far from historical reality on this one. The knives were significantly bigger, probably sharper and were used for managing food as well as enemies. The blade facing the fellow diner could have been perceived as a direct threat.

Your hands should be on the table – I am not sure what are you plotting down there and what you have in your hands covered by the table cloth. This particular rule made a U-turn in England after gardening became a hobby of choice and literal back-stabbing stopped featuring high on people's daily agendas. Dirty nails where allowed to stay off the radar. Hence in the UK, unlike in France and many other countries on the continent, you can keep your hands on your knees between the courses.

Cleaning your fork with your knife well above the plate didn't look very peaceful either and could have been a prelude to something more sinister. That's why today rules prescribe to do it discreetly on the plate only. (Clayton, 2007, S. 75).

And never ever talk with your cutlery – for the same reason. Unless you want to intimidate those next to you. It still looks pretty scary. Playing with edged tools has never been recommended.

Another example of safety demanded by European table manners—loud sounds are scary at meal times. Who didn't reflexively turn their heads when the clumsy waiter unfortunately dropped a pile of plates on the restaurant floor? Possibly, many years ago those, who didn't pay attention to the loud repetitive sound of angry knife hitting the table, were thought brave (or plain stupid, depending on circumstances). Today we try not to turn our heads unless the sound is really scary. Who would like to humiliate already embarrassed creature? Sill hitting your crockery with your cutlery or producing any other unnecessary noise which could be easily avoided, is frown upon

It is not only physical safety of people that is addressed by table manners. Just a few examples: safety of dress is provisioned by napkin. Safety of good mood is guarded by

table talk rules which prohibit raising subjects which might make people feel uncomfortable.

Given the current developments, we overall are significantly less inhibited today to discuss politics and religion at the table than our parents were. Who didn't talk about Brexit during the summer of 2016? We can even ask about house price as everyone knows that you can look up anybody house's price on publicly available property websites.

At the same time I found one new trend getting stronger and stronger. Questions like "And how is your family?" disappear from business related social functions unless you know the person really well and are totally sure that there are no divorces, no illnesses, no teenage troubles or anything else which might upset your counterpart. A couple of decades ago this seemed to be a much more common question.

Another relatively new trend is the strict rules of safety etiquette for children's parties. This has been also fortified by the growth of "no win-no gain" lawyers. It is not only that the host can be sued over an accident or inappropriate food served or dubious entertainment provided, but the latest developments also involve British mother issuing a bill to the invitee's parents for the child not turning up to the party and threatening to sue them if the bill is not paid. People responded with some new rules of etiquette aimed not at increasing children's happiness and enjoyment but at saving the parents unnecessary peevishness. One of these new rules is "Don't invite lawyers to your kid's birthday party" (Wendy Donahue, 2015). Or give other people's children a miss.

There are also safety rules for old crystal. While you are supposed to hold your white wine glass by stem (safety of wine's temperature – less chances to warm it up), if you are lucky enough to have your wine served in old crystal glasses, you are not only allowed, you are strongly advised to hold it by cup/bowl, and never by the base. Crystal stems are getting very fragile with age. I first heard this on a rather important family celebration from my grandmother, but a second too late. One item off a list of family assets.

While many people hit their glass with knife or fork during dinner to attract attention of fellow diners, it is seriously frowned upon by etiquette gurus.

We have talked already about respect to the chef and your own palate above. But in terms of safety, table manners would suggest not to offend the chef or other food related staff in any thinkable way. Being an enthusiast of respect principle it never came to my mind till I read in the book that there might be some rather serious reasons for not offending the chef. Don't cut off your nose to spite your face. Below is the quote from this book and I refuse from any further comments on this issue.

> *"Tris' reckons you should never send food back. The chefs spit on it," Jill says. "Not always," Tristan laughs. "It's not unknown. But I don't. And didn't."* (Alexander, 2014)

A lot of research is done into "comfort eating." Food used as a means to bring yourself at ease with a dangerous world out there is a well-known and well explored phenomenon. Knowledge of and adherence to socially accepted rules around the table serves pretty much the same purpose – eating becomes more predictable and hence free of unnecessary anxiety. A strict regimen, certainty of what happens around the table adds to the feeling of safety. Sometimes literally.

Last year I talked to a man whose job required a lot of travelling to countries less known. He praised the table service

at the place we had our lunch. I couldn't see anything particularly special there and asked "Why?"

> *"Isn't it good to know from which side of you the plate of hot soup arrives? It significantly lessens your chances of turning unexpectedly into the wrong direction and hitting with your elbow the waiter's hand at this crucial moment. Boiling liquid on one's lap is not the experience anyone is looking to. And trust me, I've been there – it doesn't make you popular either, especially if it is somebody else's lap your food ends up on."*

All these interesting ways you have to pay for a privilege of being a globe-trotter. And no napkin can keep you safe.

It is your responsibility as a host to make sure nobody gets ill at your table. It is your responsibility as a guest to take care of your personal safety and inform the host about your allergies. You can go as far as bringing your own food with you these days.

And if you are a host – don't roll your eyes. Whatever you think about new emerging manners, this one is not that bad. A couple of years ago I had a poor couple at dinner, too polite to mention anything in advance, but both suffering from severe sea food allergies. Well, it was summer, it was hot and we were in Croatia, on the shores of Adriatic. They watched the food on the table. I inspected my fridge trying to find an appropriate last-minute substitute for a thoroughly thought through party menu. I wished they brought fries and ketchup with them.

Guests with their own food can actually save you a penny or two. Not only on foodstuff, but on legal and medical bills. An American I met at the airport lounge waiting for connecting flight told me a story about his classmate who developed some light allergy symptoms to some common food ingredients no host would even think of mentioning. This classmate seriously had an idea to make his living by just visiting dinner parties and then claiming the damages. He gave up on it when he learned that a) you have to inform the host first – this would amount to getting hardly any food whatsoever; and b) it is only his widow who really can make some serious money out of it.

Restaurants in many EU countries have now a list of capital letters after the name of each dish on offer informing the visitors of all possible ingredients one could be allergic to (Food Standards Agency, 2016).

The list of abbreviations is provided in small print somewhere at the end of the menu. This is possibly one of the very few really good bureaucratic ideas. It clearly adds value. Each dish on the menu looks so much more important now with all the letters after the name. Lamb cutlets in special sauce, MA (Mustard and Gluten-containing grains). Trout with bean terrine, DP(hil) (Fish and Lupines). But personally, I would refrain from ordering a "Chef's salad, DAMN" (Fish, Gluten containing grains, Mustard, Sesame) (Gumpoltsberger, 2015).

Another, rather exotic and not necessarily applicable to ordinary life example of safety function of table manners, suggested by one enthusiastic fan of "Spooks."[5] Safety of pretend identity. Table manners as a give-away. Think 007, think James Bond. If you see a person with a whole piece of bread in one hand eating soup, you could be sure – Eastern Europe. Even if he has a perfect American accent and knows all the tutors in Yale. Being a proper spy means doing a bit of homework, table manners included.

ALEX KOSH

Table Mementoes. The shiny perks of high-class dining

It is not your everyday invitation. Get ready. Double check the dress-code. Triple check. Do some searches online – no more monochrome mistakes of the 90s.

All right, some humiliating details about that. I said already, that it is some sort of a horror book. Personal little horrors, but still. I was invited to a Magna Carta anniversary celebrations held in Canterbury, UK. Procession and then dinner. Black is always safe. I did go for the skin colour analysis exercise based on Bauhaus theory. My complexion type allows me to wear black non-stop. I don't do it in the mornings though. Hence the natural choice is black. It is dinner afterwards, not breakfast. Okay, a little bit of white. Just not to be boring. I am fully dressed and even like what I see in the mirror. Doesn't happen often, as there is always some room for improvement. And no, I don't suffer from perfectionism. Just a little bit of healthy longing for making every day better than yesterday. That doesn't happen often either. Procession went fine. And it's not that I didn't have time to change. It simply didn't cross my mind that somebody's colour scheme of choice could be other people's uniform. And here I am entering the restaurant, waiting to see where I should be seated, heading to the right table and immediately getting the order. "Love, could I have a glass of water please?" I needed two afterwards. And something stronger.

No mistakes like this today. The evening is going to be perfect. I am on a mission – I promised to write a feature for some publication about this place. It is outstanding. The food is said to look as good as it tastes. And all of the reviews you see are in superlatives. And the publication pays my bill! Doesn't happen often either. I even started the feature. All the history, all the facts I managed to Google. It is my day today. And tomorrow will be better.

I order judging by names. Not my usual habit, but everything is a bit unusual today. They say that all is good here. "But the fancier the name is, the more interesting is the culinary adventure," tell I to myself. So I order the "Shiny domes" for the main course. I guess I am a bit too excited. Butterflies in my stomach turn into an urgent need to leave the table between the courses. And I have to blame my elation for hitting the wrong door.

I am in the kitchen now. In front of the table where two cooks are applying the final touches to something already beyond the mortal imagination. I can't stop watching. The butterflies are fascinated too, I believe, as they get very quiet. The cooks get the eggs peeled. The eggs don't look on a par with the rest of the masterpiece. A bit smudged and sort of ordinary. The old cook takes the first egg and put it in his mouth. Whole. Gets it out. It is a culinary Photoshop. The egg is as shiny as it gets. The most attractive egg I've ever seen. Fit for advertisement without any additional effort needed.

Butterflies in the stomach wake up and demand immediate release. I leave the kitchen. The shiny domes stay on the table untouched when I ask for the bill. I pay the bill myself. And never finish that feature for the magazine.

Chapter 5. A Table of Joy.[6] Pleasure Amplification.

To feel good around the table, feeling safe to be able to eat and digest the food is necessary, but not sufficient. You don't need to conduct a survey to name two most enjoyable human activities, food and sex. Both are of paramount importance to survival of the species. The urge to check Facebook is developing, but it is still too early to say whether it would be rank 1 or 2 or remains 3 in the nearest future. (Let's see what happens when artificial intelligence takes over. Power socket manners might become a part of school curriculum).

Epicurus was right: we all wish to minimise harm and maximise happiness. Even if both definitions differ from one social group to the other. While simplified understanding equals his view with hedonism, in fact his philosophy has much more in common with stoics (Duignan, 2015). I guess many of us are familiar with a feeling of happiness only the proper fulfilment of duty could bring.

When it comes to dining, there are certain duties to be fulfilled out of respect to yourself, to fellow diners and to your own well-being. And yes, it is all about maximising our happiness by creating a table of joy through amplifying our pleasure.

As we all know good enough is never good enough. Amplification of food enjoyment is not unique to humans. If you ever had a dog, you are familiar with "burying" habits. Whenever there is enough food around, dogs would make some "reserves," burying meat and bones for a rainy day. Even if they live in the city flat they would manage to find the most impossible places to hide their food. I know a man, who many

years ago made a very brave decision to marry a woman with a little temperamental dog. He moved in and one of the first tasks on his list was to make friends with the erratic pooch. Shopping for tasty bones became his favourite pastime. He knew he made it when one evening he went to bed and found the tastiest bits hidden under his pillow. He proudly saw it as a sign of respect, appreciation, and acceptance confirmed by "sharing." I do suspect that in this particular case it was more of a fitful and rather selfish creature (yes, I met that dog too) taking care of itself – making its own food taste better.

"Dirt also served as Mother Nature's refrigerator, keeping buried bones fresher longer by protecting them from sunlight. This natural "aging" made the bone tastier too." (Moore, 2013)

Salt, sugar, spices, and various food additives, different cooking techniques are used by humans to make food more flavoursome. And yes, we do age our steaks too before cooking. But we went a little bit further in food enjoyment enhancements – when we eat, we make not only our taste buds work. We engage all our senses and a brain in making simple a "re-fuelling" act a wholesome occasion to celebrate. Enjoyment of food is a multi-sensory experience.

We make food the centre of this celebration. Many table manners are actually aimed at preventing us from taking our attention elsewhere.

Pleasure amplification is always beyond manners and rules of fine dining.

That's why we remove all the bad smells before dinner and are trying not to use air-fresheners with a chemical smell. We would rather boil some apples with cinnamon or roast some coffee beans.

That's why it is considered to be a bad manner to have TV switched on while eating, or have the radio on with any other programme rather than some smooth undemanding music. You wouldn't like to have Elliot Carter's Drammatico as your dinner choice. Believe me, I tried it once. Or Spotify it for yourself to see what I mean. It takes you away from the dinner table in no moment at all. Carmina Burana is not a good choice either for the same reason, although in a rather different way. The latter at least doesn't undermine your feeling safe. You are less likely to jump and drop your knife at a culmination point.

That's why we like having a separate dining room not used for any other purpose, if we can afford one. It is essential for good eating as much as a proper designated bedroom is essential for a good night sleep. Nothing to distract you from the main purpose of being there.

That's why light in the dining room should be enough to properly see what is on the table. Nice looking food makes our mouths watering before we even touch it. But if it is too bright, we start seeing other things, which could leave befuddled and disturbed, like cracks in the walls or particularly unappetising portrait of an ugly ancestor in the corner.

That's why we dress up for dinner. But out-dressing the hostess or wearing the same dress, even worse in my book, doesn't add to her or to your joy. But I have to say, it amuses the onlookers.

That's why certain unappetising topics are excluded from dinner conversations.

That's why we like solidity of shiny silver in our hands and a nice feel of starchy napkins to make the occasion special and to reinforce our pleasure.

That is why the rule of white is in place for good dining. The table linen for dinner, if you choose to have one, is always white.[7] So are the napkins. And the same goes for china. Minimum decoration, minimum distraction. Food presentation benefits when the background colour is white. Yes, you can have more colour for breakfast and lunch where less effort went into food and event preparation. But not when you really want your guests to appreciate the food and occasion to the maximum degree possible.

That is why the plates with Winnie-the-Pooh on them might be instrumental and even invaluable in getting toddlers through that porridge, but have no place on the formal table, unless it is an A.A Milne themed occasion. The best wine glasses are clean and clear with no embellishments.

That's why there are so many rules for table setting.

* The settings

What we see on the table is of high importance. European etiquette doesn't leave any room on the table for things unnecessary. It is not only for hygiene reasons we are not allowed to keep our bags on the table. There is no place for a lovely little purse with embroidery there either. Even if it is sterile, it doesn't add to food enjoyment. It takes attention away. Frills distract. Distractions lead away from the activity. Pleasure lessens.

Of course, it is all culturally shaped and depends on expectations based on previous experience. What perfectly works for some people will not necessarily work for others. If our (positive) perception of how food is served, of crockery and cutlery used, confirms our (positive) expectations, food is perceived as tastier and more expensive. (Vanessa Harrar and Charles Spence, 2013). It works the other way round too, I assume. A long time ago I had to work for a couple of weeks in a foreign country where the only eatery in the walking distance from the office served coffee in a plastic glass. Sugar was in the bowl on the counter. There was only one coffee spoon available. It was chained to the counter next to the sugar bowl. The pack of milk next to it was fixed with a long rope. I had my coffee black since. No milk, no sugar. Thank you.

Tradition of lavish tables in time of food scarcity in post-communist countries could be explained with joy delivered simply by quantity of food. Tradition required all food to be on the table at the same time, especially for starters with at least 4-5 varieties available, the more the better, so there was hardly any room left. A spacious table with enough room for every guest and hardly any food on the table itself, all served in restricted quantities individually and in specific order, were an exceptional rarity. And seemed somehow suspicious.

ALEX KOSH

Food, served on the table or in a different way, as long as it is according to the liking of the group eating, always brings joy. And if the quantity and quality are not guaranteed, scarcity of it could also amplify enjoyment of the very moment of consumption in a rather masochistic way. Especially if anticipation of the next meal of a similar quality doesn't have a particular time frame to it. You value your spendings more if you don't know where the next pay-cheque is coming from.

It is only when the lower needs (physiology and safety) are satisfied that a meal becomes an art and a real joy. And it starts with the table. As the title of this chapter, Table of Joy suggests, it has a bit to do with maths, especially with the beauty of proportions.

It is recommended to have at least 60 cm (2 feet) between the centres of the table settings to keep guests comfortable and properly served. The table should be a masterpiece. It should be "geometrically spaced" (Arthur Inch and Arlene Hirst, 2003, S. 20).

Some butlers use a ruler or a measuring stick for perfect table setting. If you ever watched "Downton Abbey, you would know what I mean. Or you can use a rule of thumb suggested by Nicolas Clayton (Clayton, 2007), recognised English authority when it comes to table manners and a professional English butler. As we all know from school, proportions are important for the table of joy. Especially, if it is a cutlery and crockery alignment.

"An elegant, formal dinner is one of the most joyous ways we have to commemorate special occasions, and a brilliantly set table makes all the difference" (Arthur Inch and Arlene Hirst, 2003, S. 17). Tableware, an important element of beauty of table, developed over centuries. It followed and sometimes even demanded advances in technological and industrial progress of humanity.

Over the course of years, humans developed not only suitable materials for cooking and serving (the most obvious clay, silver, glass and china), but also different shapes of tableware to bring the best out of food and the most beautiful setting to the table. There is a wonderful book, called "The art of the table" which extensively covers the history and the modern state of this matter (Drachenfels, 2000). Food does taste different depending on presentation and today's ongoing extensive research on role of tableware in our taste guarantees that one can expect some further developments in this area in future.

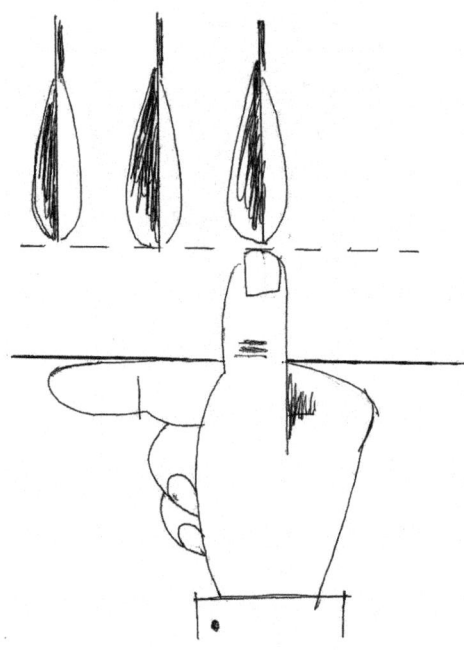

* The company

We invite people to share our meals with us for a variety of reasons. It is a bonding exercise, it is a way to say thank you; it is a tradition we sometimes question but still follow. It could be a comfortable setting to discuss uncomfortable issues and it is business time spent efficiently. It could be even a way to ask for favours. My partner and I are always invited for lunch by a lovely young couple when they need a lift to or a pick up from the airport. Parking there for two weeks, when they go on holidays, is more expensive. They might even bring some presents from exotic destinations afterwards. Lunch doesn't have a "thank you" function in this case. It has a "please" function. It works. Call it corruption, but we never said no to my partner's kids. Don't tell them though that we would do it without lunch either.

Whatever is the reason of sitting at the table with other people, we do expect the experience to be nice and enjoyable, healthy and safe. This goes without saying. Unless you have a difficult relative you **have** to invite (and who hasn't), we expect people we invite to contribute to the pleasantries of eating together. We do expect people to exercise certain level of control over their behaviour and adhere to the rules and manners requested in our social group. This includes basic manners regarding Health & Safety. Health and safety of conversation is expected too.

A good deal of mishap is based around conversation. Asking inappropriate questions, saying wrong words, dwelling on a topic considered inappropriate... You name it. Wrong fork never helps, but is easier forgiven and forgotten than "*Oh, you live in London? Where do you get all the money to afford it from? Do you have a rich man to pay your bills*"?

But is not only safety we expect. Not being offended is not

enough. Safety is a prerequisite to a nice dinner, but not the major request. We expect to be entertained at the table

The history of humanity is full of great conversationalists. Churchill, Isaiah Berlin, Mme de Staël, Samuel Johnson, to name just a few—although one has to admit that table talk proficiency was not the main reason for them entering the posterity. But still it was quality important enough to remain in history.

The rules of verbal exchanges have been studied since people moved their conversations beyond the basic minimum of exchange necessary for survival (The Economist, Special Report, 2006). The rules are under constant scrutiny. Look at the book shelves in your nearest book store.

In pursuit of pleasure amplification, we expect the dynamics of conversation; we expect unexpected (pleasant) twists and witty remarks. We want to enjoy the atmosphere around the table. We want our guests to contribute to joy. We want to laugh. And not after the party, over the dishwasher remembering this and that. We want to share laughter at the table the way we share food. And it is not about good mood only. . Laughter is good not only for your mood, but for your stomach too (Shere, 2010).

Whether a conversation around the table is pleasurable depends very much on people around the table. It is easier to have good times with people sharing your concept of what is enjoyable and what is not.

> *"Finding the balance between politeness, or should I call it suitability, and wittiness is sometimes an issue. It is good to have "Cards against Humanity" type of jokes with some friends and you have to quote James Joyce non-stop with others. I personally don't like French dinners neither for having to watch half of the process,*

[8] nor for the need of verbal acrobatics" – says an American writer of German origin.

The most difficult table talks to manage I've ever been a witness to myself, were the regional meetings dinners in Balkan region where Serbs, Croatians and people from Bosnia-Herzegovina would be seated next to each other. A Serbian girl told me that this could be a huge effort for everyone to keep the evening pleasurable.

> *"There is a very dangerous line you wouldn't like to cross in conversation between sharing your good things and traditions you have in common in the region and moving closer to discussing history, especially modern"*

I never understood what she really meant till I had to sit down for business lunch with a group of Russians in May 2014 after Russia annexed Crimea from Ukraine.

It doesn't help anyone or anything to deliberate at the table over really serious matters to which you are prone to react emotionally if and when you can't laugh about them. If you can't laugh about it, you can't discuss it either. You can't win the cause, you don't contribute to the solution and it doesn't help your food absorption either. Making friends is not an option in this case either.

And yes, there is room for humour in the toughest situations possible. But you can deploy it only when the basic needs of safety are satisfied. When you are with well-mannered people and the knives are turned inside the plate. If you cannot afford entertaining different groups of incompatible people separately, then seating plan is your next best answer. Just make sure that no one plays with the name cards.

Violet Crawley, Dowager Countess of Grantham:

> If you can all put your swords away, perhaps we can finish our dinner in a civilized manner.

Isobel Crawley:

> But I admire it when young people stand up for their principles.

Violet Crawley, Dowager Countess of Grantham:

> Principles are like prayers; noble, of course, but awkward at a party.
>
> ("Downton Abbey:", IMDb users, 2010-2016)

ALEX KOSH

* The Role of Rituals

Rituals and manners around the table have many functions. Each social group has a system of rites, however small. For the enthralling analysis read Margaret Visser (Visser, 1992). Pleasure amplification is a very important but often underestimated function of rituals.

We value "easy" things less. Easy comes, easy go. Who cares? People spend lottery money differently to the same amount resulting not from luck but from decades of saving. The words "The idea of waiting for something makes it more exciting "are attributed to Andy Warhol but the feeling is known to anyone who grew up in a family where birthdays and Christmases were celebrated with presents.

This is exactly what rituals at the table do. They allow us to pay tribute to food, to those who harvested and delivered it to us, to ourselves for being able to afford it on our tables; and they make our food taste better. Since 2013 this is official (Catherine Saint Louis , 2013). Even silly and absolutely not relevant to food and eating rituals like, for example, knocking twice on the table before taking the carrot, then knocking twice again before actually eating it, do the same. They make the carrot taste better.

Somehow this research makes me think about Pavlov's dogs and extensive salivation when hearing the feeders' steps. Anticipation augments, saliva glands swell. And every step of the food-bearer lessens the barrier between the food and the stomach. In further research of reflexes, some of the dogs were taught to press the pedal (or something else equally meaningless) to decrease waiting time. And they happily obeyed.

This is what, I believe, rituals are about when it comes to consciously increasing food enjoyment. An (artificially created) barrier ("Not presently, darling"), heightened anticipation, participation in making a desired thing happen – all resulting in amplified enjoyment when we finally reach the goal, food in this case. Random actions, gestures and words do not have any influence on taste. Regulated and repeated in strict prescribed order - do. But don't overdo it either.

Disclaimer: don't kill the joy of anticipation. There is a powerful psychological trick to cope with unhealthy cravings – just imagine the whole process 30 times or more. All the details, the taste, the feeling of satisfaction, the pleasures derived and the award achieved. The allure washes out gradually. Eating chocolate 30 times in a row makes you tired. And if your imagination is vivid and you use it to its full potential, the attraction of the vice significantly diminishes if it doesn't disappear altogether (Borreli, 2016). Be careful. Don't imagine your next Christmas dinner more than a couple of times.

Participation in ritual is another important condition. Research, mentioned above (Kathleen D. Vohs, 2013) reported no increase in taste amplification for those who didn't participate in the ritual. While I fully agree with the general statement, I am not sure about the example chosen by "The New York Times": "Another experiment found that watching someone perform a ritual, say removing the wrapping on a wine bottle and uncorking it, does not heighten a spectator's relish of their glass of zinfandel — only the pleasure of the bottle uncorker is enhanced." (Catherine Saint Louis , 2013)

That's not how I feel on the evenings when my partner brings a bottle from his cellar, gets the glasses out and we move closer to the fire place. Watching the cork pulled out does the trick for me. There is always room for passive participation.

ALEX KOSH

* The great offenders

Food enjoyment is killed when our senses are not satisfied or worse, are offended.

When the restaurant you are invited to smells of burnt onion or of poor drainage system. Or both. Happened to me when the owners where trying to sell me their premises as a seminar location.

When touch feels wrong: when your steak knife is too light and feels like useless plastic.

When you see a cockroach making its way to the larder.

When you feel that there is some sort of judgement about the way you eat.

Or when table talk takes an unexpected sinister turn.

Enjoyable dining experience is what everyone expects when going out. But even in good places you could find a major offender of dining experience. I don't want to touch here the obvious cases of blunt food and bad service. It is obvious. But noise is another matter. The majority of people would not like to go the empty deserted restaurant with no ambience and to work like advertising by being seated by the window.

If you are going out for dining, not clubbing experience you also expect a possibility to engage in some greatest experience enhancers - enjoyable conversation. Unfortunately, it is not always possible. Everything which stands between a diner and his enjoyment of food causes moaning if not hunger induced rage.

Below is an excerpt from interview with one diner, particularly sensitive to noise, but it perfectly describes the views of many people I talked to.

Of course, the younger people are, the more tolerable they seem to be to the excessive noise.

> *"I hate loud music. Where does the habit of restaurant owners come from to have music which kills every kind of talk? Is it to cover the noise of cutlery permanently scratching the plates? Is it to make people leaving right after they have put their cutlery aside? Is it to make them drinking another bottle of wine to get deaf and resistant against the unbearable hubbub? "*

It is not only the loud music diminishing our enjoyment. The manners of other people disturb us too. From another interview:

> *"Loud eaters are scary. I was with friends in a posh restaurant enjoying my meal as well as the perfect service in a wonderfully designed place. Everything exactly to my liking. Could have been the adventure of the year if there were not a table of most likely half-deaf people with especially noisy cheer- leader. A voice like an entertainer live on stage unplugged. We are not into our meal any longer and are not able to keep the conversation among friends going. Everybody is exposed to the outburst of the table neighbours. You are lucky if those comrades speak the language you don't understand. You would not understand a word and could focus on your own small talk by just tolerating the noise in the background. To get ready, let's spend some time at the Zoo next to the roaring lion's cage before the great lunch meal."*

And the noise doesn't have to be loud.

> *"He really enjoyed his soup: slurping it from the spoon and making some sort of a cat purring sound after every slurp. I couldn't eat any more."*

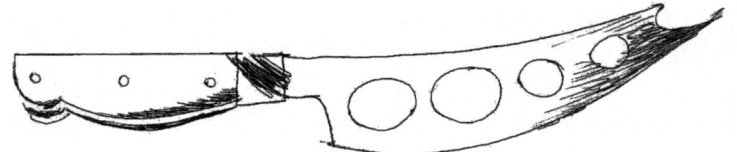

The way people eat, their table manners are another great enjoyment killer. And even more, it seems, if eating happens in places not specifically designed for food consumption. It takes away from food's significance in our lives and diminishes respect not only to all the effort which went in harvesting and preparation, but also to ourselves and people around.

We all had to eat at our office desks at some point in time. But if this in encroaching on other people private space, like strong spices smell, you could be seen (or, rather, smelt) as a killjoy.

Eating on public transport, I was told, is never a great idea for many reasons, not to mention hygiene and safety. What if the driver pushes his brakes and you choke?

Today it seems there is a new threat to it: you and your snack can become a web-based amusement for thousands in a couple of tube stops. It is a rather popular worldwide trend today to take pictures of strangers eating on public transport. The most famous in the UK is a subscription only Facebook group called "Women who eat on Tube" (Sanghani, 2014).

It has been a subject to wild criticism. But that's what the owner has to say: "Well, according to founder Tony Burke, it's not stranger-shaming; it's the London equivalent of wildlife photography. "At its truest form," he says, "it should cherish its subjects in the way a wildlife photographer cherishes a kingfisher in a river." Burk believes the trend he created is art (Sanghani, 2014).

This Facebook group has often been criticised as sexist. Those, who organised back in 2014 a protest against this Facebook group, often say they feel intimidated by strangers taking pictures of them.[10] Most of them are perfect illustrations to "how not" and are rather convincing if you ever needed a reason to assure your teenage daughter that she doesn't need to snack in between meals. But it is not only men who take photos of eating women. Many women happily contribute to the visual collection and to the heated discussion too.

When this discussion was at its height, I talked to an elderly lady living in a picturesque village not far from Canterbury. Her cottage windows have only heavy old curtains which are drawn only on cold night when the heating is on. There are no net curtains or blinds and during the day all the passers-by can see her pottering around the house, reading in the arm chair next to the window or eating at an old table. I asked her whether she minded other people watching her at home. She didn't understand first what the problem was and then laughed saying

> *"Darling, I grew up in a house where there were many people around who didn't belong to the family. You just went to the bathroom or to your bedroom or to that scary attic if you ever wanted indulging into something you minded other people seeing."*

The same thing but from another angle was explained to me by an American telecom consultant when I was running a research project for one of the first private telecom deals in Europe. It was many years ago, when mobile phones were much heavier and less common, but the potential for what it would do to our concept of privacy over the next couple of decades was already there. He said that with the advent of mobile communication life literally became an open book. And the only rule for survival is *"If you feel uncomfortable, don't do it. If you chose to do it, stop worrying."*

When people complain about loss of privacy today, I try to imagine how private life was previously, when towns and villages were smaller and everyone knew nearly everyone else. There were strict mechanisms of social control in place

(Boundless, 2016). You would always pay your bill if eating out. If not today, then tomorrow or on you pay day.

Everyone would know who you are and whether you have paid. Today people threaten to put CCTV of customers who went for a runner on Facebook. Or actually do it. (Dean, 2015) It works. They pay even if with a limp excuse.

With anonymity of megalopolis and certain social formations being destroyed or significantly modified, society is desperately searching to replace effectively and appropriately old forms and means of social control. Virtual space is as good a platform as any.

Don't expect new social control mechanisms or the self-appointed judges to be welcome. There is a great rule I've learned in consulting business – never ever offer unpaid professional advice. At least not at the dinner table. There is a reverse rule in etiquette of table manners: when seated next to lawyer or doctor, don't try to solve your problems for free. If only some etiquette professionals knew the consulting rule.

My friend, a successful exporter of tiles and sanitary ware from Spain shared a dinner with me and an etiquette teacher. The latter, a lovely lady in her sixties, wanted to be helpful. She watched my friend's cutlery handling and then advised her to do it differently. The friend went red and took her knife inside the palm. Whenever I invite her to dinner now, she apologises, but still asks me every time who else will be around the table. She never did it when she held her knife as a pen.

The other, less dramatic example. We are at the conference in Budapest. Breakfast in the hotel with a view over a blue Danube (actually, it is always grey or green. I never saw it blue). A woman with a wonderful posture eats her bacon with fingers. My colleagues can't help watching it, trying to break crusty bacon with knife and fork. Bacon escapes. The lady turns to the man whose bacon just made a somersault on his plate. "I am an etiquette consultant," she says. "It is OK to use your fingers." Obedient students we are, we put the cutlery aside and deploy our fingers. All watching the Danube.

Next morning, without much of the discussion all three of us go to the breakfast table out of sight of any potentially very helpful voluntary advisers. No difficult food on the plates either.

We express ourselves through our table manners. We learn them subconsciously when we are very young. If the person never ever came to the point in life when they decided to change their manners intentionally (getting a "paid for" advice), criticising one's table manners or giving unsolicited advice is similar to bluntly saying "I find your jaw line disgusting." This doesn't add to joy around the table. We revolt. More on this in "ID" chapter.

* The menu

The role of menu in increasing the joy of the table is well known. There are special rules about what follows what to make sure that our palate doesn't get bored and keeps contributing to happiness even if we have to clean it with sorbet or special crackers in between. Fish is not served after meat, cheese is kept for finale (and not for starters) – you can get the full list of guidelines in many etiquette and cook books.

There is some room for experiment, but you need to check it with your eaters first. It is not the properly cooked and well-presented insects (Goodrich, 2013) per se if everyone is aware what they have been invited to, which would keep your guest from coming to you again. It is their lack of anticipation and a shock of a properly cooked fly in pasta if it was left unannounced on the menu. Respect your guests. Don't make them feel scared.

I visited Kazakhstan on business seven years ago. We were the clients to the local research company. The best and the most interesting part of business travel after getting your job done is to see the country and get an inside feel to it. Most of my business trips fall into a well-designed, procurement-approved, safe and boring scheme: airport, taxi, hotel, office, taxi, airport. So I cherish any moment.

Kazakh people are really friendly, polite and perfect hosts. The best barbeque I ever had was there, at the open-air place high in the mountains with a breath-taking view over Medeu skating ring (over 1600 m above sea level).

In the evening we were invited for dinner and a folk show in the restaurant in Almaty. Eating in a place you've never been to before is always a bit of an adventure. Even in your own country. You are never safe even with the most traditional dishes. You never know what really will appear on your plate at the end – will it be according to your expectations? Would the crust on jacket potatoes be crusty enough? Is mash smooth and butter like, or would you be presented with some potato crumbs? And it is even more of unknown abroad. Sometimes you cannot even make any sense of the name of the dish or of it (translated into English) ingredients. "Assorted ice-cream" in local language could be magically transformed in "Ice-cream, ass." in the English version of the same menu.

Of course, there is no chance I can understand what baursak, djai, talkan, kazy or shelpek mean. The best I can do is to go audacious and just put my finger randomly on the menu. And then enjoy my luck or total absence of it. Why not to let the hosts choose? And then we share. The hosts are delighted. It is an opportunity to show us the best. And they do. They order something looking like a sausage. I ask what it is. They answer. When I can think again, I develop a couple of very personal table rules for myself. Never ever look a gift-horse in the mouth. Or anywhere else for this matter. Never ever ask what it is. And never ever compare anything you are offered to what it reminds you of. Even if you are sure it is exactly what you think. You might end-up in jail[11]. I was saved by my well brought up and brave junior colleague. He ate it all after seeing my face. And no, he didn't ask for a day off on his return either.

One of the very powerful ways of making the menu more enjoyable and highly awaited is to have it seasonal.

Pleasure amplification involves certain control over consumption of any sort. "Too much of a good thing could be wonderful" is one of the most famous Mae West quotes (Curry, 1996), but it is not only hangover after too much of wonderful champagne which makes life less tasty. It is overconsumption of anything.

ALEX KOSH

I used to live "out of suitcase" for a while. This means you never really "unpack" when you get home. You take the dirty laundry bag out, replace the items with similar (sometimes identical) clean ones, see if you still have tooth paste left, print out the next boarding pass and off you go. The worst month was the one when I visited 7 countries on three continents. My younger friends thought it was fabulous. I dreamt of the moment when I would be able to afford to take all my suitcases to the bulky rubbish collection.

A psychological experiment proved that "abundance of desirable life experiences may undermine people's ability to savour simpler pleasures" (Quoidbach et al. & Jordi Quoidbach, 2015)

Eating "out-of-season" food has never been in favour with gurus of table manners. First of all, it was not available all the year round in the past. Second, even if it could be stored, the storage conditions were not perfect, so it didn't taste the same. All of this is not true anymore. We can have what we want when we want from wherever we want. But still the "out-of-season" menu is seen by many with disdain, and for the environmentally conscious the concept of food miles, how many miles food travelled before appearing on your plate, is another great advantage of the seasonal menu.

McGrady, the author of "Eating Royally" book and the former chef in the kitchens of Buckingham Palace says: "You can send strawberries every day to The Queen during summer at Balmoral and she'll never say a word," McGrady said. "Try including strawberries on the menu in January and she'll scrub out the line and say don't dare send me genetically modified strawberries. She absolutely does eat seasonal." (Gruenwald, 2016)

Wonder what is when in season? If you live in Britain, you might enjoy the book, first published in 1920 by J. Rey under the title of "The Whole Art of Dining with notes on the subject of service and table decorations" and successfully reprinted by Oxford University nearly hundred years later, although as an abridged version (Bodleian Library, 2013). There are plenty of other advice there illustrated with amazingly decadent examples of fine dining. None of the "Great Gatsby" themed dinners I attended a couple of years ago would come anywhere close.

Benefits of seasonal eating are plenty. "For starters, it connects us to the calendar and often to one another, reminding us of simple joys — apple picking on a clear autumn day, slicing a juicy red tomato in the heat of summer, celebrating winter holidays with belly-warming fare. Secondly, produce picked and eaten at its peak generally has more vitamins, minerals and antioxidants than foods harvested before they're ripe and then shipped long distances. Eating seasonally often means eating locally grown foods, so it's good for the environment too: It supports small and midsize local farmers, cuts down on pollution from shipping and trucking food and reduces your carbon footprint. And if all that's not enough to get you to make some simple switches in your diet, consider this: In-season foods save you money" (Cleveland Clinic , 2016).

The main benefit of eating "seasonally," when it comes to joy of table, is anticipation. As with rituals, waiting for certain food to appear on the table again, after a long "looking forward" period, makes asparagus or tomato or oysters, you name it, taste better. "Christmas everyday" is a sure way to deny yourself a simple joy of living.

Table Mementoes. Thank you for the invitation.

I invite an extended family of my partner for dinner in a trendy restaurant outside Vienna. The restaurant's website claims it is well posted. And yes, there is a sign next to the exit from motorway. Just getting into the right lane is a bit of a challenge. But we are there. At least that's what I think for the next fifteen minutes. Till it becomes too difficult to fool myself that we know where we are going. According to the GPS screen we are in the wild. No roads, just blank grey on the screen. The tired lady of GPS even stopped urging us to make a U-Turn if possible. But there is tarmac under the tyres. And some traffic signs I can hardly make any sense of. So it is not the end of the civilisation. Not yet. "Frogs on the road" as a matter of fact says my partner. "Don't they have them in England?" I don't know about England. I live in North London when not travelling abroad on business and work on the Thames bank. Yes, I do go outside London. To Oxford, Cambridge or Liverpool. Clearly no "Frog crossing" signs on Archway road or on M1, swear. But it rings the bell. I read something about taxpayers in New York country hopping mad about their money spent on the new signs during recession. "Who would slam the brakes" the discussion went. "Would you really hit the brakes if …" I ask. "Of course, I will. I always do" he says. I am out on this one. But frogs are safe - I don't drive either.

After additional half an hour of wild straying in the country the voices from the back seat start. Kids. "Never trust advertising and GPS." There is something in the old proverb "The hungry man is an angry man." "We should have taken that turn, I told you" the wife of the hungry man joins in. "Is your name Google?" replies the driver. I am grateful they don't ask "Are we there yet?" But I think when you approach thirty you don't need to spell this one out. You can figure it for yourself.

We find ourselves on the narrow lane surrounded by Vienna woods and its old trees on both sides. The restaurant turns out to be very well posted once more. You neither can miss this second sign nor can you turn back or take any other road. Here it is, a poster with some illegible scribble pointing up the hill. Everyone in the car sighs with huge relief. We thought we were totally lost in this tiny narrow serpentine lane, fortunately totally deserted now as there is no way for two cars to pass each other in opposite directions.

We park somewhere locals in my car consider to be a car park. There is not enough light for me to double-prove it. Many things are based on trust in life. Even if my heels, deep in the muddy turf urge me to be less gullible.

Somewhere at the end of the restaurant's green, under the lamp post the old lady is waiting for us. My partner's mother. Turns out for the last half an hour. She doesn't have GPS or Google maps. She just drives in the area for the last 50+ years. And has all her paper maps properly laminated. It rains quite often in the hills, as hikers in Scotland would definitely know.

We are 40 minutes late. But they have kept the table. It is not a huge sacrifice though. I can only spot a couple in the corner. Both on a liquid diet. Little do I know how much I would understand their choice in a couple of hours.

In addition to be well posted the restaurant prides itself on outstanding molecular cuisine and modern interior design. They can add "progressive table service" to this list too.

We are shown to the table with Buddha ceramic statue in the middle. Somehow spontaneously the old lady and I start rearranging the cutlery – turn the knife so that the blade is not to the right any more. Put the fork from the top of the charger to its left. Move the spoon from the left to the right. We both know too well you shouldn't touch the table arrangement. You don't move the host's furniture when invited to the place where the design ideas foreign to your own reign, do you? But somehow uncontrollably I am looking around trying to spot the place where the sculpture can go. I will put it back on the table myself. After the cheese, promise. It turns out it will be after the sweet fish mousse. But who cares. Apparently the kids do. They follow my movements with ceramics in my hands with poker faces. They recently bought a bigger statue in Ikea for their garden. Buddhas are in vogue these days.

The waiter appears. And yes, I did expect some sort of a glove service. White-glove-service which you would normally associate with class, ambiance, grace and upmarket environment. And everything else they promised on the website. What I am not fully ready for is "just-one-black-left-hand" mitten on the waiter's hand. The old lady is quick to comment "You can save a lot on washing this way. Shall we visit the place where the right-hand mittens went to next time?"

The five course dinner is a perfect illustration of things going interesting when the name of the concept is interpreted literally. Molecular turns out to be, first of all, about the size of the dish. The one-hand-black-gloved waiter is not very articulate when asked about cooking methods. But very helpful – without him we wouldn't have been able to tell what is what. It all tastes pretty much the same.

We go back to the peaceful darkness outside. The old lady says "Thank you for…" and then obviously struggles. You can see her re-winding the dinner. And then she smiles. She found the point she could be sincerely thankful for. "For the invitation," she happily finishes the sentence.

I make a mental note to book something central next time for her. Somewhere in the 1st district of Vienna, close to Stephansdom. Where everyone can get a taxi to. And where liver pâté and chocolate on the menu are separated by page, not by coma.

Fast forward. Couple of years later. We take my English friend for lunch to the same place. No Buddhas, no mittens, no empty tables. New chef, new waiters, and a new menu.

Chapter 6. ID rules. Psychological and sociological background.

This is where all the fun starts. We are proud of our manners and we are afraid of being judged on them. We want to be seen as having refined manners and we are not ready to take unsolicited advice. We do not allow strangers to say anything about the manners of our children but happy to criticise the parenting styles of others. We publicly state that is doesn't matter how you hold your knife; it is more important that you are a good person realising your full potential. And at the same time we raise our brows at those who eat from their knives. Manners maketh the man. Or to be precise, they definitely define what other think about that man in the making. Manners help us put others before ourselves and they help us achieve our own goals. They help us feel superior but also help us interact successfully as equals. They enable our smooth gliding into new, more desirable social status and they hold us back. You can take girl out of the village, but you can't take the village out of the girl – the saying very popular in Russian speaking circles when societal change of the late eighties and nineties dramatically increased social mobility in post-Soviet countries. And table manners are no exception. On contrary, they are in the avant-garde when it comes to social identification.

"Not knowing how to eat 'properly' is universally a sign of outsider status. Proper eating includes the kind of food used, the way of preparing it, the manner of serving it, and the way of eating it. The intricacies of the tea ceremony are known only to the Japanese; social climbers in the West can be spotted immediately by their inability to master the details of place settings; "using the wrong fork" is an offense as grave as

spitting in public. Since anyone wishing to integrate himself into a group must eat with it, there is no surer way of marking off those who are in and those out than by food etiquette." (Robin Fox, 1999)

The problem with table manners is that the first time we learn them, we have no idea what we are learning. We learn table manners the way we learn to speak – just following the little herd of these particular skill bearers which in majority of cases happens to be our family. As kids we absorb table manners with whom we eat, we listen to and follow the instructions without any judgement, at a blissful age when parents are still gods and can do no wrongs. One of our basic needs is to belong to a social group, to feel love and appreciation. It all starts in the family and nothing can frighten us more as kids than losing your parent be it in a busy place or in our imagination. And if they tell us "That's how we do it," we are more than happy to oblige. We want to be good girls and boys. We want to belong. We want to be loved. There is nothing wrong with this – this is how we learn to survive and thrive in a big world out there, full of "others," when handholding is not provided anymore. When we have to use all the skills we picked up on the way to adulthood to ensure we flourish. And this is the reason why table manners are so powerful in social pigeonholing and judgements on who is in and who is out.

We often hear about importance of stable environment for children. Moving from one set of rules to another is confusing. An old adage "your children should see only the things you want to see in them" is still working. This is also the reason why there is no such a thing as etiquette for children only, despite all the numerous books and manuals selling well on this subject. There is no point in telling 3- or 4-year-old that you should say "Hello, how are you? How was your day?"

when someone comes back home if all he or she hears from their parents on their return is "What's the mess?!" You can't explain to a child that his mother does something wrong. And under no circumstances should you.

Books on kids' etiquette sell to parents with the clear awareness of the need, and in majority of cases looking less for the rules per se, as they know already most of them and practice them daily, but rather for techniques to build up these skills in their children in a more efficient and a more sustainable way.

What I am still to come across, is a proper, psychologically sound book with a title along these lines: "How do you teach your children all those important things your parents forgot to teach you?" I'll buy a few for all the kids in my life. And one for myself.

* Social identification.

"Us" and "Other" is possibly the oldest and still most powerful social division we have. It exists on all possible levels and in all imaginable sizes. This is "us," which unites couple in love in contrast to everyone and everything else. This is "us" as a family and everyone else not sharing our genes. This is "us" as a group of friends and others who, being neutral but given a chance, might become our friends ("us"). And the most distinct otherness— known adversaries if not enemies.

The group of "us" could be huge when we talk about national or ethnic identification. It could be quantifiable like in "all 252 residents of Northern Road are united in their protest." Or no one would have the faintest idea of how many of "us" are out there. We, people with good table manners... We, who know how to lay the table properly... We, who like to barbecue in the park...

We use pronoun "we," like I do in this book, to show that we are not alone. That there are other people who share our thoughts – this gives credibility to the latter. This gives an individual some standing in the society and some confidence in communicating the views to others. If I write that "I believe good table manners are of outmost importance" it is very easy to ask me "And who are you?" It is much more difficult to question the importance of using a napkin if I state that "many people with good table manners are convinced that civilised dining involves linen napkins." (Honestly, it does). You are less likely to argue with many of us even if the one presenting the views it is still the same old me.

The need for belonging, of course, also has "survival" function, both historically and today. Belonging is impossible without being accepted, without being "loved" by the group. This is the need familiar to and longed for by overwhelming

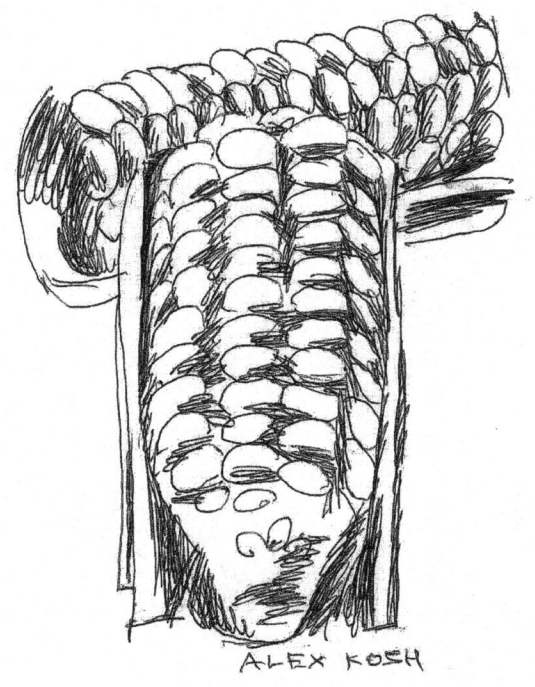

ALEX KOSH

majority of people. Happiness is derived from the feeling of voluntary belonging more often than not. Even longevity is a function of happy social belonging according to the results of the longest longitudinal survey, Harvard's Grant study (Vaillant, 2012)[12]. That's why we are in constant search of approval. We want to be loved.

> *"Eating with the cutlery was the easiest way to be a good boy when I was little. Not only in the eyes of my parents, but also their friends were impressed. The father was particularly happy to take all the credit, although I don't have any memories of him being at the table often"* said an Egyptian man, currently living in Vienna.

He also told me that in Egypt to be seen as educated and being properly brought up, you should totally refrain from finger usage. Whether it's bacon, asparagus (finger food in Britain) or pizza, which moved to finger food even in Debrett's recent book published (surprise, surprise) by Pizza Express (Furness, 2012), educated Egyptian would eat it with silverware. According to the Telegraph's[13] poll 32% of readers of their online edition still object to eating with fingers in the restaurants (Furness, 2012). Jay Remer, more known as The Etiquette Guy from Canada, a consultant and columnist specialising in International protocol and corporate etiquette, made the following remark on the newspapers page: "As a traditionalist, I am very disappointed in Debretts. They've slipped on the proverbial banana peel!" But there was much more discussion about licking fingers than tradition. Modern manners move on.

So, there are "we" and there are "others." Those, who use their fingers and those who never do. It would be too hasty to say that usage of fingers is invariably connected to the lower classes and this recommendation appearing in Debrett's

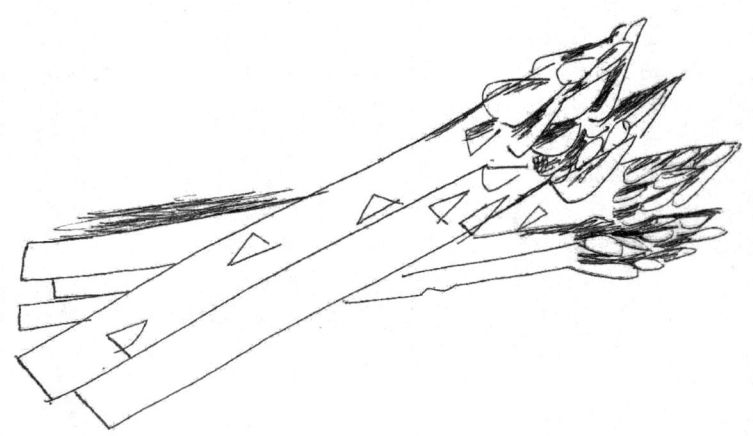

(authority in British etiquette) is a clear sign of democratisation of manners. But you are safe if you say that usage of fingers at the table is a good indication of person's personal ID. It all depends whose fingers they are and which food they touch.

"Asparagus is hardly a vegetable because it's got a sex and class life of its own. Certain Sloane hostesses faced with unknowns still see asparagus as test. Humorous upper-class men have been known to ask for a knife and fork" (Ann Barr and Peter York, 1983, S. 58). This is an example the subtleties which differentiate "us" from "others" as soon as we end up at the same dinner table.

Moving up and achieving a new social status is often reflected in all things table related. We want to send a signal to the outside world about our new identity. And we use all the means available.

We all belong to a number of social groups – family, work, social networks, hobby related organisations, social class, ethnicity and citizenship to name just a few. And birds of a feather flock together.

"Others" are different. They could be just ever so slightly different, say, some cousins with exotic foreign mother. Not "us" when we talk about the immediate family, but still us when it comes to broader definition. They could be similar. Unknown yet, but trustworthy hence with an obvious potential to become "us." It is interesting, that people who look more like us are perceived as more trustworthy. It is not only about language and speech, clothes, behaviour and, of course, table manners, it is also about facial features. (Royal Holloway, University of London, 2013)

Others might just have the same mother tongue and hold the fork just like we do. They are clearly "us," when we meet them somewhere in Mongolian deserts even if we would never call them when back.

"Oh, this photo? It's a family we met on holiday abroad. They were fun. We spent two weeks together. I wonder what they are doing now. We haven't been in touch since after."

Others could be threatening, whether they present intellectual, physical, financial, moral threat. They could be neutral. And possibly boring. And there could be "others" we aspire to.

To change social identity upwards without inherited wealth and social status one needs to change quite a few things: get relevant education levels, find better paid job, create relevant networks, move to a more desirable area, just a few examples and this list is not exhaustive. The boot-strap theory is still popular among many people in the US. This list of necessary actions is very long and some points are easier achieved than others. Consequently, it is easier for those who want to move up to start with external symbols of the group one wants to join. Clothes, the way they speak and, of course, the way they eat. It is easy to observe the difference and it seems to be easier to implement.

In the modern world of global corporations, upward mobility and career progression very often involve a long-term assignment abroad. If there is no well-established expat group of similar nationality, the ambitious new-comers are most likely to try to adopt behaviours of the upper local social group available to them.

This is also the case when people move to the country for good and are willing to adapt to the new home rules. They are not necessarily your traditional economic migrants from poorer countries – in many cases these are people who are searching for safer place for their money and some more predictable and reliable surroundings for their children. London, Berlin, New York and many other cities today are full of young people speaking a language one can hardly define. It is Turkish German where Genitive case does not exist anymore. It is Russian with majority of English words in it. It is Ukrainian enhanced by Canadian intonations and a mixed English/French vocabulary.

Another problem with changing your social identity and joining the group you aspire to, is that those who are already there, and especially those who believe that they own this particular group, don't necessarily want you fully in. As a table manners related example, I have been told by someone at a corporate function after someone tried to use a neighbour's bread plate: "Well, it's a bit too late to learn what is what on the table in the middle of you career. He can only hope that he doesn't sit next time to someone with a bit of manners and some decision making powers."

This is where the concept of teaching etiquette and manners, table manners included, enters individual life today. This is why Kate Middleton was apparently taking classes in Royal Etiquette (Everett, 2011)

Etiquette helps a person to move ahead as it is seen as the proverbial boot strap, helping people to reach the social group they want to be associated with. Profitable etiquette teaching business today is mainly about geographical mobility and social climbers.

"Ms Messervy of the English Manner, consultancy on etiquette and things related says: "we started benefiting enormously from the fact that so many international people were coming to London to live and work. Those that sought us out wanted to learn how to better integrate into the culture." She added that many of her clients come from Eastern Europe, China and the Middle East, as well as India. "They want to get in with the right people professionally and personally and be accepted," she said. "But they also want their children to fit into the culture." (Conlin, 2014)

"A lot of the new foreign money here is horribly ostentatious," Mr. Hanson said. "We want them to learn that having money does not get you everything you want; you actually have to behave well to get ahead." He added, "We just help speed things up for them if they have not had the benefit of an old-fashioned granny like I had in my upbringing." (Conlin, 2014)

I have also met a few etiquette teachers working with their immediate surroundings rather than with high fliers from abroad. It is a bit more old-fashioned. The lady I talked to is more interested in making her immediate world a better place. Dinners – more enjoyable. Children – less irritating. A trip on a bus – less stressful. She might find some new money ostentatious but it applies to her local neighbours too, on a smaller scale though. No yachts in sight. She teaches at local schools voluntarily, they run church groups and/or local/ regional clubs. She writes columns in local newspapers. But it looks more like a hobby she is quite lucky to enjoy due to inheritance from her auntie.

For etiquette teaching to become a thriving business the teacher also needs to present appropriate background - a grandmother with impeccable manners, a lover with title, a relevant job experience with those, who are seen as unquestionable carriers of good manners. But even better – an own mansion with some properly trained staff around (this is still a rarity among etiquette teachers). It is also desirable to have some knowledge and skills, and regular access to suitable experience. It is impossible to teach someone how to eat and

what to expect at the formal function if you've never been to one. It is impossible to teach manners for eating out if the last restaurant you went to ceased to exist a few decades ago. But most importantly you need two things on the clients' side: a real need to get in and a bit of fear to be left out. This is where the money is.

A French man with some business interest in the UK told me:

> *"You will never belong. You will always do something wrong. If you know how to eat peas with tines down, you will find out that you don't cut your Christmas Turkey correctly. But they will be very nice to you as long as you pay the bill. And they will always talk behind your back."*

Well, a proper upper class advice then from Violet Crawley, Dowager Countess of Grantham (Downton Abbey): "If I had withdrawn my friendship, from everyone who had spoken ill of me, my address book would be empty" ("Downton Abbey:", IMDb users, 2010-2016).

* Fear sells.

While the positive effects of upward mobility are very well known and appreciated, "on the negative side, a high rate of vertical mobility may produce individual and societal <u>anomie</u> (a term coined by the French sociologist Émile Durkheim). The individual experiencing anomie feels socially isolated and anxious; in a larger, societal context, generally accepted beliefs and standards of conduct are weakened or disappear" (The Editors of Encyclopædia Britannica, n.d.). Which means a little personal drama – despite achievements, the person doesn't know anymore where they belong. The major human need is left unsatisfied.

The majority of people need to belong and be appreciated, and very often in case of upward mobility this leads to search of new social identity, not only externally ascribed on a new business card, but also internalised by the person and accepted by the new social group the person has entered.

Social anomie is difficult for the individual as it removes the known rules and routines of social behaviour. Norms of behaviour which were automatically and successfully applied yesterday don't work anymore. In extreme cases they could become counterproductive, not only preventing you from "gliding in," but also exhausting your energy well before you manage to do something really meaningful. On an individual level it makes a person rationally seek for the best solution in the most mundane situations. It keeps your brain busy. They fear losing it all by something which in their eyes is no fault of their own. For example, it can turn the simplest act of eating together with your new equals into a hazard.

A Czech lady who moved to London when she was 18 shared one of her difficult memories:

"If you didn't smoke, than the best place to socialise with

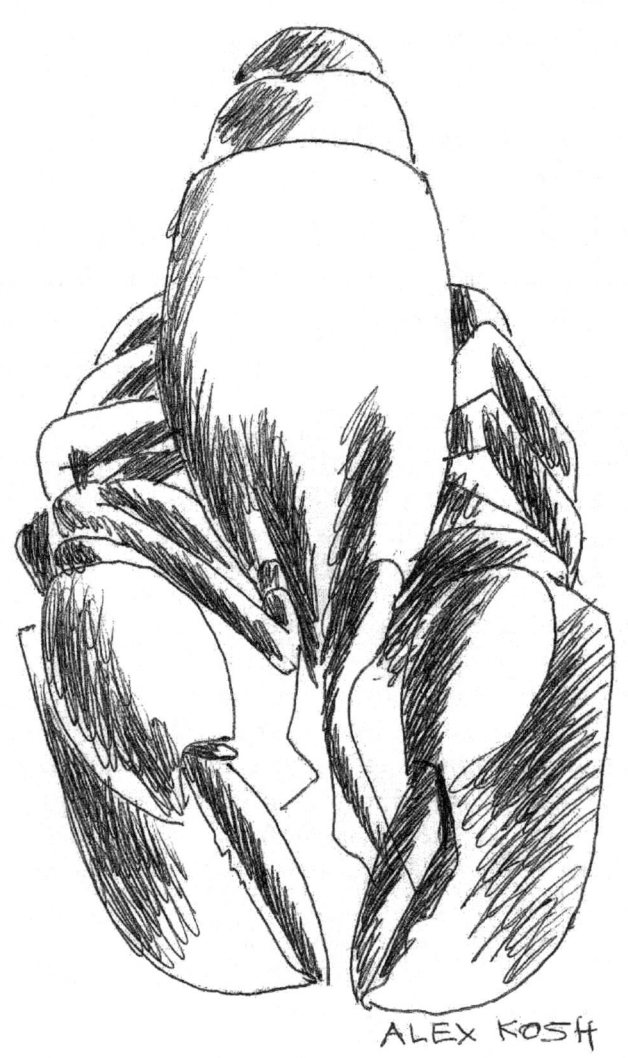

ALEX KOSH

your colleagues would be lunch at the canteen downstairs. I wouldn't go into details and tell you how I ate and what I did, suffice to say – nothing criminal or immoral, but it was enough for all of them to keep staring at me. I stopped coming to lunches and ended up feeling rather isolated."

"Our thinking and our behaviour are always in anticipation of a response. It is therefore fear-based" (Chopra, 2016).

You don't need to watch "Mad Man" to know that fear sells. Bird flu is one of the best examples for me. I once talked to the CFO of one of the big international companies. He said that he bought enough bird flu vaccine for all his senior managers when he read headlines in his morning newspaper that the dead swan was found in the lake not far from the office. Possibly bird flu, the newspaper claimed. Couple of days later, in a much smaller article, on a page with a double figure number, they explained that the swan was killed. The neck was broken. But vaccine was already ordered and the extra storage was booked.

"It doesn't matter what I am afraid of. Be it winter flu, or BO, or some FOMO (fear of missing out), or anything else, you name it – just offer me THE solution. Tell me how you can make me safe. And I would be much more willing to open my purse, driven by this maddening feeling that if I miss the solution, my life will never be complete. I won't be able to fulfil my potential. Nobody would shake my hand" - said a former French colleague of mine.

She is in unique position; she has an insight in how it works. As a market researcher she did a few projects helping advertising agencies to select the most efficient communication strategy. But still, she admits she falls prey to those strategies.

Image and etiquette consultants successfully sell exactly on this premise. You will find in many books and on many etiquette-connected websites phrases like "Gliding in" – not being left out; rude behaviour will hinder your business; when we don't follow etiquette or don't know the rules, chaos ensues; bad manners might cost you your job, don't wear thongs because if you have an accident the emergency team would know immediately how lady-like you are (possibly meant as a joke but the advice is given seriously)." I deliberately don't quote the sources here. They are just typical of many more, possibly better examples you can google for yourself. Humour is often used to dilute scaremongering tactics, but they are there. Many etiquette courses employ video-recording of students before for analysis purposes and criticism. It works. Not many people like seeing themselves on photos. Even less watching themselves on video. And I am still to meet someone who likes his or her own voice when recorded.

Fear creates the need for etiquette courses. All the etiquette teachers I ever talked to, say that it is impossible to teach anyone who has no interest in table or any other manners.

These are different type of fears. For the person it is a fear of not fitting in; of not matching the expectations of the family, of his or her bosses, peers and social group. Of not being as polished and sophisticated as one could/should. This requires a certain amount of ability to self-reflect which is crucial for any type of self-development (McConnell, 2010), even if it is not seen as self-improvement.

Parents don't want to be seen as parental failure when going out with children. For managers and their bosses this could be fear of not knowing the rules hindering your act. "Classes in "corporate health" in the United States now include sessions on "How to Read a Wine Label" The rationale is that without such knowledge corporate executives may be subject to "stress" which would impair their performance." (Robin Fox, 1999).

Not all jobs pressures resulting in need for etiquette classes are orthodox and upfront. "Girls are sent 'to etiquette classes, to learn how to sit, eat, which knife, fork, which glass for the white, for the red. It can't be obvious to the other dinner guests that she's a prostitute.' It sounds very My Fair Lady - albeit a pornographic version." (interview with a high-class prostitute. Tatler report. (Edwardes, 2014)

So even if there is no personal need to "get in" to start with, it could be created by bosses and by peer group. Or by personal mishaps. "Having learned business etiquette the hard way (ask me about the night I spit spaghetti on my boss's tie), I realized I had to get business etiquette right." (Freedman, 2016) There is a reason behind top decision makers, including Obama and Zuckerberg, preferring the same type of outfit every day. (Baer, 2015) Making too many minor decisions get your bran tired quicker. As mentioned before, you cannot keep negotiations going if you have to make constantly minor decisions like whose bread plate it is, where do I put a napkin and what is this for.

There are not that many people in the world for whom table manners are the major instrumental factor in satisfying the top human need in Maslow's hierarchy of needs – self-actualisation. But there are many people who when reflecting would admit, although often playing it down, that table manners play a certain role in satisfying their need for self-esteem. Nobody would like to be seen eating as a pig. "Higher emotions are what separate us from the lower orders of life... higher emotions, and table manners." Deanna Troi of Star Trek, The Next Generation (Quote, 2016).

Selling etiquette on fear could be possibly seen as contradictory to the whole purpose of etiquette of making people feel better in each other company and eliminate eventually any negative feeling in social interactions. "The best type of etiquette is to make the other person feel they can do no wrong," (Ruiz, 2015). More on paradoxes of etiquette in the final chapter. Need is created by situation reflected by individuals, pressure is added by bosses and peer groups, and etiquette teachers are happy to oblige with "horror examples" (to which I am clearly contributing with this book). The type of fear which sells etiquette is fear of risk. Fear of doing something wrong and trying to prevent it. Fear of the wrong fork.

"Of course, fear of risk is actually the bestselling tool of all: it is the basis of the entire insurance industry, whose profit base is predicated on the fact that fear is a very real emotion selling the product, but the statistical probability of anything actually happening, well, that is infinitesimal. Fear through risk sells us a product we don't even use. Genius." (Peretti, 2014)

Nobody wants to risk the wrong fork when they have already put a lot of effort into making their world their oyster. Even at the age of five.

> *"The other day my five-year-old son refused to eat a slice of cake because the fork he'd been given 'wasn't a proper cake fork'." (Highgate Mums, 2015)*

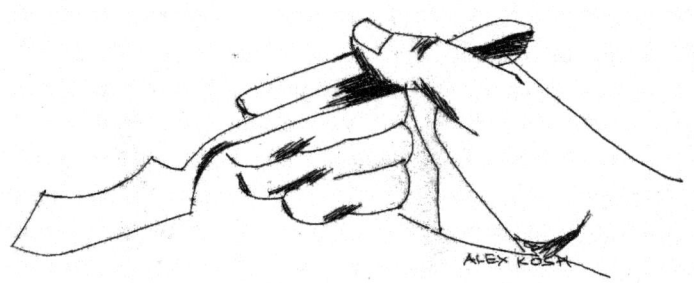

* Gut Factor

Do you know that feeling when you are instantly sure something is wrong, but you would not be able to offer any meaningful explanation if asked "why"? Or have you ever had the feeling that this is the right and the only possible course of action, but you can't put in words any rational reasoning behind it?

Intuition, gut feeling, "and then I knew"– all these are the words we use for "sudden, strong judgments whose origin we can't immediately explain. Although they seem to emerge from an obscure inner force, they actually begin with a perception of something outside—a facial expression, a tone of voice, a visual inconsistency so fleeting you're not even aware you noticed." (Flora, 2007). In our case these are table manners. Some people believe the gut feeling is originated in the gut itself, as there is plenty of rather recent research proving the gut has "a brain on its own" (Carpenter, September 2012). Others believe it is the result of a brain work. The origin of insight in this context doesn't really matter, although I definitely would like to know for sure whether I have one brain or two. Wherever this sudden insight comes from, it is understood currently as a quick procession of all the facts available to human being in question in order to select the most probable or the most beneficial solution/ possible course of action or simply to provide the rational self with the basis for further consideration. Emotions are inseparable part of this process.

"Intuition," says Linhares, "can be described as 'almost immediate situation understanding' as opposed to 'immediate knowledge.' Understanding is filled with emotion. We don't obtain knowledge of love, danger, or joy; we feel them in a meaningful way." (Flora, 2007)

Good instincts rely on the rules of thumb (heuristics) when only the most important information is taken into account and everything secondary is discarded. (Gigerenzer, 2007) When we dine with someone who doesn't belong to our usual social circles, we just understand that the person in front of us is not one of us, even if we have common interests and common friends in place. Then we have to mind our words and behaviour to prevent any potential miscommunication. The set of rules of dealing with those who are "in" is different to prescriptions on how to deal with those who are "out."

Normally we never think that we know this because of his or her table manners. But historically, table manners different to ours could be threatening even if they would only signify the wrong choice of potential partner. It is less of a case now, but the instrument to warn us of potential dangers survived.

In general, gut feeling is a great psychological mechanism, as those who lack it are virtually paralysed when it comes to too much information and hardly any time for scrutiny. As any human type of social analysis it involves judgement. And if we can deal with and modify accordingly the judgement we arrive to by long rational exercise, the instant feeling is another matter. It is a basis for further rational consideration. We have a feeling of what it is; now we can think what to do further.

An accountant with the offices in London and Switzerland told me about his first lunch with one of his international clients.

> *"The man didn't talk with his cutlery nor spoke while chewing. He would put his cutlery back on the plate in between. The problem for me was that he would pick up the next bit of food on his fork before putting it down on the plate. I am not used to this. It is rather distracting. I had to make an effort to follow the conversation."*

As always, life demands balance – we are less productive if not able to make intuitive judgement and need more time to rationalise. We are less competitive in our decision making if we rely on guts only and cannot consciously take all the factors even if they are outside our usual experience but are crucial for developing the right course of actions. The more experience we have of certain things, the better is our intuition in this area. And we hardly have more experience in any area, than dining habits of our social group. We might have not enough experience of another social group, but we have enough to judge in a second who is in and who is out. And we rely on our gut response whenever we meet "others." This is a historical safety mechanism allowing us to get ready for flight or fight before it is too late. They are not always correct if based on irrelevant experience but they are there and it is not that easy to decide whether it is right to ignore them or not.

One of the women I interviewed told me about meeting her new boss at the coffee break at the company's conference. She didn't like the spoon which never left his cup, not even while he was sipping his coffee loudly. She said that she should have trusted her intuition rather than dismissing it as fevered imagination.

> *"I should have looked for a new job straight away. The years of bullying which followed, were awful!"*

Chapter 7. ID rules continued. Your fork is not your shovel. ID markers.

* Country

Table manners as markers of social identity are present in social groups of all sizes. The most known and the most obvious ones are the differences between the countries or even the continents. This is a prolific ground for jokes and stereotypes. The abridged edition of "The Whole Art of Dining with notes on the subject of service and table decorations," by J. Rey (modern title "How to dine in style"), written nearly a hundred years ago, in 1920 has a very historically interesting chapter on "Table manners and foods of the nations" (Bodleian Library, 2013). This chapter seems to describe nearly every nation the author ever met and leaves you in no doubt about the nationality of the author. Before quoting, it is worth reminding that this book was written just after the Great War World War I). Ridiculing someone else's table manners could be often the way to channel more profound dislikes of "others" through on the face of it more guiltless observations.

> *"(about Germans) ...by the way they flourished the knives and forks, anyone might think they were fighting a duel with swords! One of them alone, when he is eating, makes more noise than twenty Englishmen together; and when a party of Germans is in a restaurant, the band cannot be heard while they are drinking their soup... The Austrian and Hungarians, though having much in common with the Germans, are of much finer type and style, and their table manners are decidedly more refined...The Russians are not yet quite*

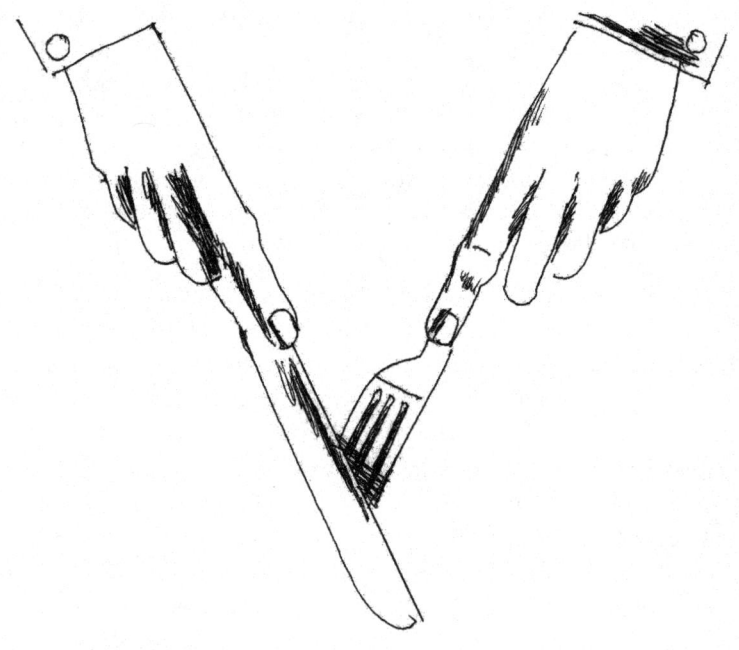

up-to-date with matters concerning the table...The Brazilian and the Portuguese people have much in common regarding their food...With regard to their manners at table, the less said about them, the better." (Bodleian Library, 2013, S. 99-100)

While the world moved further to globalisation and convergence, *including* to some extent convergence of table manners, profound differences between countries are still in place. So are the stereotypes and ridicule. I was surprised to learn that some Americans believe that nobility in Britain drinks its tea with a little finger propped up "Contrary to mockeries of British aristocracy, "you would not need to pinkie-up." (Ruiz, 2015). Even if it ever was the case, of which I still need to be convinced, it is clearly frowned upon now.

The first thing you learn about table manners when you move to Britain is that "the fork is not your shovel" which means that you are never-ever supposed to turn your fork "tines up" or hold it with a "shovel grip" (with index finger next to your other fingers, not at the middle of the fork's handle). Despite Americans calling this "Continental style," the actual continental style is different. Austria, Germany, Central and Eastern Europe hold the fork in the left hand like Americans do – like a pen. "Using a fork correctly is the same as holding a pencil. The child balances the fork on his middle finger with the index finger and thumb on top." (Richey, 2015). "Tines up" are perfectly legitimate.

The major difference to American style is that "zig-zag" (putting the knife down and taking your fork in the right hand) is not allowed. But there is more or less unanimous agreement across the countries in Europe and across the pond that holding your knife as a pen should never ever be learned or practised.

I had two young Austrian interns staying with me for a couple of months. One of them asked me for tips on food-related matters. Both accepted the pub etiquette rules (Fox, Passport to the Pub, 2016) without any questioning. Pub as an institution doesn't exist in Austria. All beer drinking Austrians I know are fascinated by the concept. But the fork grip was rejected for a few weeks with an argument, till the boss invited the department they were interns to for eating out. Seeing is believing. And your fellow diners staring at your cutlery technique helps to accept some advice as true quicker. You can find fascinating debates about proper cutlery grip online. But as one of my interviewees said, *"The British way is the safest one – you can use it anywhere without standing out too much."*

Where to put the napkin if you have to leave your table between courses is another great divide. There are many manners and etiquette related groups on LinkedIn. You can find a heated napkin discussion nearly in all of them. While many Europeans and English in particular can't imagine the napkin anywhere else rather than on the seat of your chair, other countries are very happy to see it on the table or hanging on the back of the chair (with all the food related stains cheerfully on display to fellow diners. You now know where I stand on this). One of the arguments presented in those LinkedIn discussions for the latter still puzzles me. Apparently, a few contributors claimed, the seats are dirtier than the back of the chair, touched by dozens of hands per day. Not only because restaurant menus, lemon and lime wedges and salt and pepper are much more dangerous, if you believe Forbes (Cohen, 2012) and seats are not even among the top ten offenders. No. I am just wondering what forces you to eat in the place where you cannot trust basic hygiene standards neither for furniture provided by the establishment nor for clothes worn by customers.

* Class

Class and table manners is another well researched area. As mentioned previously, a search for pleasure and beauty amplification gets to its full speed when the basic needs are satisfied and you don't need the napkin rings to save on laundry. There is a very strong association in people's mind between nobility and desirable table manners. The interest in table manners among the majority of population is inspired by this. Parents often call their children "my princess" or "my little prince" (this happens less often though) in many countries in Europe and beyond. Although there are social lifts and even real Cinderella's stories around, sane people clearly understand that to have blue blood in your veins you need at least a bit of it in your ancestors. So whatever your manners are, inclusivity will not be granted here. You are either in and part of an extended family, literally, or as the majority of us – out.

Interestingly enough, sanity is sometimes nowhere to be found on a huge scale if history gives you chance to re-write your own.

After perestroika the new money in post-Soviet country were relatively easy. Markets opened and opportunities were plenty if you had a bit of imagination and desire to persevere. Whatever money people made by running even a tiniest business was in huge contrast with previous years of deficit and total employment which hardly paid even for basic necessities. New money always looks better with a bit of patina.

An old relative of aristocratic origin was a proper icing to the new bank account. The fact that many archives were destroyed after the revolution helped. Suddenly it seemed that everyone was a descendant of someone handsome and noble. All those

workers and peasants, freed from serfdom only in 1861 officially but never really, those, who "won" October revolution, they disappeared. Possibly, they were too busy with building communism to have any children.

We become able to strive to satisfy more sophisticated needs, like need of self-esteem and belonging to the desired social group, when the "lower needs" are already taken care of. It is difficult to follow the rules of pleasure amplification when you are still not sure how stable the quality of your food is. Whether you will be able to afford the same dinner tomorrow. That's why nouveau-riche culture around the table and outside of it demands crutches – all you could do to show and reaffirm your financial achievements. When they are new, they seem to their owners (and often are) fragile. Subconsciously one seeks reassurance that this is not a dream.

Proves of accomplishment are on the table not even necessarily for the guests, although them appreciating the hosts wealth and achievements would be a bonus. It is more for the hosts themselves in many cases. Frills on the table are there to prove to everyone, themselves including, that they arrived. In this case the joy of table and enjoyment of food are derived from quantity and price tag attached, rather than quality of experience. The more secure you are of something, the fewer reminders you need that it is there.

Connection to the inspirational social group is often used to give one credibility when it comes to table manners and to etiquette in general. Grannies, lovers and relevant experiences ("When I was invited to that exclusive...") are used as social crutches for desired authority, even by some, especially self-appointed etiquette teachers. Association with imaginary (or not in some cases) nobility in the family somehow seem to justify snobbish criticism, but in fact the upper class manners

are not necessarily always those which would be seen as good by lesser mortals.

"The food you eat often indicates what class you are. The way you eat it, namely your table manners, does so almost more. The upper classes, for example, don't have any middle-class inhibitions about waiting until everyone else is served: they start eating the moment food is put in front of them. This stems from the days when they all dines at long refectory tables and if you waited for fifty other people to be served, your wild boar would be stone cold" (Cooper, 1999, S. 255)

I read this after a year of frustration. A woman, whom I really respect and admire, has been staying with us several times for a couple of nights in a row. There would be an evening when after sightseeing and long walks I would brace myself and cook something. Serve the food and then go back to the kitchen to sort out some minor things only to come to the table to find out that she had already nearly finished. I couldn't understand why this human being I really adore can't wait.

My partner said that she was relaxed and behaved as her normal self, as if at home. Even if Jilly Cooper wouldn't have written anything else (and she produced quite a few of amusing reads), I am eternally grateful for this paragraph above. It restored my faith in humanity.

This book also provided an answer to another table manners' puzzle I had. It did bother me for many years why a certain elderly lady whom I met from time to time for Sunday lunch at friend's house in Austria never said thank you or somehow commented on food. When on one of those occasions after particularly amazing fish (I am a lousy cook when it comes to fish myself, hence have a heightened sense of appreciation) I said that it was really good, the old lady looked at me and

sincerely asked "But what else would it be here?" According to Jill Cooper, you can hear "thank you" in relation to quality of cooking from some people only if they realise that you don't have a cook and have to do all of it yourself.

I deliberately don't touch food itself here. There is a lot of fascinating reading available on class distinctions when it comes to food and drink, such as "Watching the English" by Kate Fox or "A guide through the American status system" by Paul Fussell. It is enough to say that white wine is safe and apparently less calorific than many other drinks. And I stick with it.

Perceived table manners of upper classes could be a relatively non-expensive way of feeling closer to your dream. It is affordable luxury, the same way like perfume and make-up. But if sales of perfumes are driven by allure of celebrities, "Lear proper table manners" classes are sold by the social group we aspire to belong to. That's why etiquette is a popular topic in tabloids, especially in sections targeted at female readers. Women are more susceptible to social scaremongering (Nauert, 2006). I hate to say this, but according to some scientists, women are more envious "of the status of same-sex rivals" (Saad, 2009).

And tell me an easier way to boost your status than by replacing your paper napkins with linen ones. Perhaps, only stopping pushing your plate away after eating is finished.

Envy also plays an important role in willingness to deceit. "We find that upward social comparisons predictably trigger envy, and that envy promotes deception by increasing perceived gains and decreasing psychological costs of engaging in deceptive behaviour." (Schweitzer, 2005)

But we don't see this as a deception. We see it as "self-improvement." Still the instructions you might get from your teachers on developing the new habits would be along the lines "fake it till you make it." Hence – we have etiquette guides with the title's not only "Etiquette for dummies," but also "Bluffer's guides" (www.bluffers.com) (fun reading it is though) and "Kate-iquette" classes (Showell, 2014).

There is nothing wrong with this. World clearly becomes a better place when grace and poise are all around, and nobody talks waiving a knife in front of my face. Just possibly we can shift the focus, just a little tiny bit, from using the right fork, which is still important, to the main purpose of modern etiquette - making everyone around you feeling a bit happier. Cooks and waiters including.

Even if expression "aristocratic manners" is a rather alluring one and helps the business of selling etiquette and good manners (I know someone who still cringes when hearing etiquette and sales together in one sentence. Apologies for having done it again), it is not the table manners of nobility which have been driving development of habits, crockery and cutlery, and everything else around the table for the last couple of centuries.

Class divisions differ today from country to country, not every country has nobility, but the majority of countries have aspiring middle classes. They are the real driving force behind etiquette fads serving no other real purpose rather than social group identification within your own class or with the group you want to associate with.

* A secret language of being in

If you go to Dorotheum in Austria, the main auction house of the country, you will find millions of embellishments to the table. Just a couple of examples. Knife stands, which have no function rather than decorative one. You can't put the knife you used on it. The tiniest bit of gravy will immediately end up on the table clothes. Gravity is still in place on this planet. "Bone holders," which are tiny trays with special hooks to be adjusted to the plate.

Either poultry was much smaller previously, or they never ever were used for any other purpose than to show that you are "in the know." Gravy/sauce holders adjusted to the plates in a similar manner. While those are at least useful to prevent all of your food being soaked in sauce, especially if the latter has a rather strong taste, I was strongly advised against them and was told a couple of horror stories about sauce holders ending on the table and all the juices on the diners. While many of these things could be very beautiful in a way some figurines are, they are nothing else to the table than "decorations and cutesies" and superfluous accessories.

This is the function any other fashion has. If you can demonstrate you are fully conversant with what is in vogue, you move immediately couple of steps up the hierarchy ladder within your own social group. You are not only "in," you might even become a trend-setter.

This is not the thing of the past. I've a seen an awesome in its own, rather special way plastic centrepiece in one of the shops last year. Elaborated napkin rings, cutlery rests and (my favourite) "menu holders for exquisite dining at home" are plenty on the market. What scares me, they are really used.

My first encounter with a menu holder at home dinner happened at a dinner party at home of a successful Belgian businessman located in London. Fashionable accessorising requires special manners. "You are supposed to read the menu before indulging into conversation" I was told when ignorantly tried to start one before acquainting myself with things on the menu over which I had no say and which I would get on my plate anyway.

An American neighbour confessed that she feels much better living in London. The competition between friends in "whose table is better accessorised" she was part of at home, finished.

> *"None of us can afford a house big enough for proper entertainment. We all go out and split the bill. It's such a relief."*

Feeling good, belonging to a safe place could also be provided by inclusive table-manners of smaller groups. Many of us have small "ceremonies" we share with old friends. You know you are among soulmates and you are safe when it is re-confirmed by special rituals.

Below are excerpts from different interviews.

> *"we don't say cheers when we go out for drinks. We say "hurray." It started when we all were very young and having drinks in the pub was a real case to celebrate"*

> *"The first time it happened it was a bit of an accident. He squeezed his lemon wedge on his fish, but it escaped and landed on my plate. I tried to pick it up, but similar story. So if we are in the same company and there are lemon wedges around, nobody could resist the fun of having our lemons flying. It is not so well perceived when other people are around, but we do it sometimes just to have an "in-joke" when it gets boring."*

> *"I go out sometimes with my old colleagues. It was*

lovely time. We worked in a small company and we are still in touch and get together at least once a year. We had a boss who used to lick the knife, but was a real rock for our team. He died a while ago, but we might lick the knife without saying anything as some reference to him when we indulge into memories."

It is like a secret handshake the only purpose of which is to satisfy our need to belong and to be loved. Small social group ID table manners are there to reassure you that you are not on your own. I, me, and myself cannot not feel socially important without some of "Yous" around.

Going out and familiarity with expected etiquette in public places is another social ID marker. It is a sign you belong to the groups of population who can afford going out. It is a sign that you have someone to go out with. Unless it is a hotel with business travellers, people still pity those who have to eat alone. Food is something to be shared. It is not calories only.

"We have a new neighbour, on the wrong side of seventy, I guess. We see him whenever we go for lunch to that local place. He always eats alone. I guess his wife died recently. He clearly doesn't look like a sad loner otherwise." (excerpt from an interview)

Table manners jokes are based on inclusive identity. They are not really possible around the table with people from different background. Have you ever heard about a funny eating joke played at a formal dinner? Even if there was one, I am sure not everybody understood it. And even among those who understood hardly anyone joined in. Table jokes at formal table are not jokes. They are protocol gaffes.

For a successful table manner joke you need, first of all, to know the rules and fashions. You need to have people around the table who have the same knowledge and ideally - the same sense of humour. You need to share the language, and by this I don't mean English or German or Hindu. It was not funny at all when at my first Christmas party in England I was kicked by some flying bread. I had no idea about that old bread-roll-throwing fun. For me it was a double offence – first to me, then to everyone else, bread included.

Some totally acceptable, even required table manners might look like a joke to someone who is not in. But they are not. At nearly any ball in Vienna you will be served traditional food – sausages (often Frankfurters) with bread, horseradish and mustard. And a paper napkin. Don't expect any cutlery with it. Do you remember the Asparagus test I talked above?

Very indirectly connected to table manners, clearly literally connected to language, and somehow a food-related joke to all the English colleagues of mine were the invitations to German and Austrian restaurants with rather interesting names. You don't expect to be invited to "Lust Haus" (restaurant in Vienna) when on business trip. Not really, even if the idea had been crossing your head couple of times in some form or shape. You definitely don't expect to find good food in LoosHaus (Austria). Service – definitely. But food? And the winner was the invitation from then CEO. We had the rather serious meeting, which ended with his joyful invitation to the unprepared public: "And now we all go to Wonka!" (restaurant in Germany) Turned out to be a rather fine place. "Shall we go to Wonka" became a synonym for the invitation to go out for a meal for a couple of years to follow.

While some identity-defining table manners originated historically, there is always room for ill-conceived creativity and unnecessary attempts to create something artificial in order to re-affirm superficial sophistication simply for the sake of being different. The best known example is the picture of empty plates with different "finish" positions of the cutlery to show the waiter whether you appreciated the food or service or not. It stormed the internet couple of years ago and was even seriously discussed by some professionals. I printed it out, laminated and carried it with me for a while. None of the numerous waiters and diners I have asked knew anything about it. They also didn't find this method of feedback useful or funny.

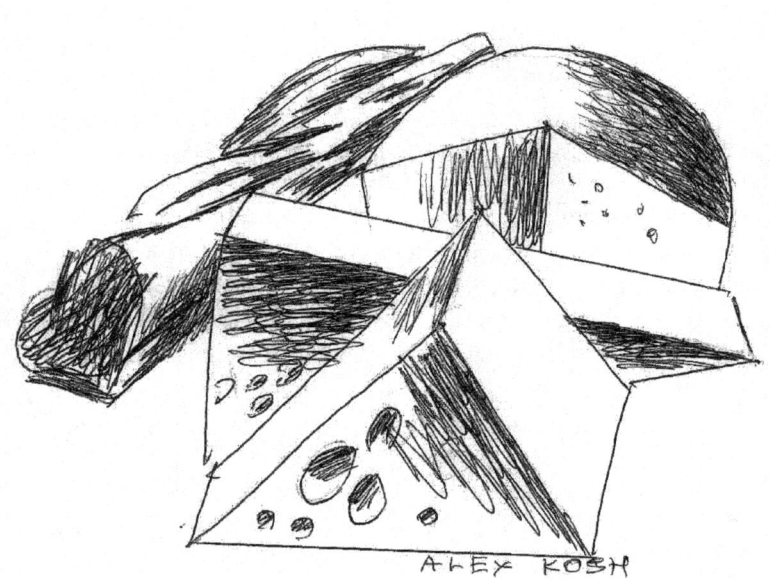

ALEX KOSH

* Table manners and politics

While association between national identity and table manners is widely recognised and sufficiently researched, the connection between table manners and political orientation is known less. The most famous historical example is Jacobite's "King over the water" loyal toast.

> *"Throughout the years of struggle in exile, the Stuarts continued to have many supporters in England and Scotland. Because their support was treasonous, the Stuart sympathisers – the Jacobites – instituted, among other things, the practice of drinking toasts to their king 'over the water' in glasses engraved with coded symbols that reflected their loyalties. Often a glass of wine would be held above a bowl or glass of water as a toast to the health of the king was offered; thus literally toasting the king over the water"* (Martin, 2013).

While I am not familiar with any modern secret table manners of political significance, even the quickest glimpse into the matter makes you suspect that it is a catch-22 issue. In voters' perception, political orientation and credibility of public figures are connected to their table manners. Eat your hot dog with cutlery, you are out of touch and pretentious. Eat your sandwich without any and you are not refined enough (Li, 2015). Or if you don't eat as an average citizen, the next you know they ask you for your long-form birth certificate (Kanalley, 2011). The lady I interviewed, who was in the past one of the candidates in the local council elections in one of the European capitals, said that she dreaded those moments.

> *"As soon as food appeared in sight, the photographers would get excited and go into constant zapping mode. You can bet one of these thousand pictures they take will be ugly. They won't use the other 999."*

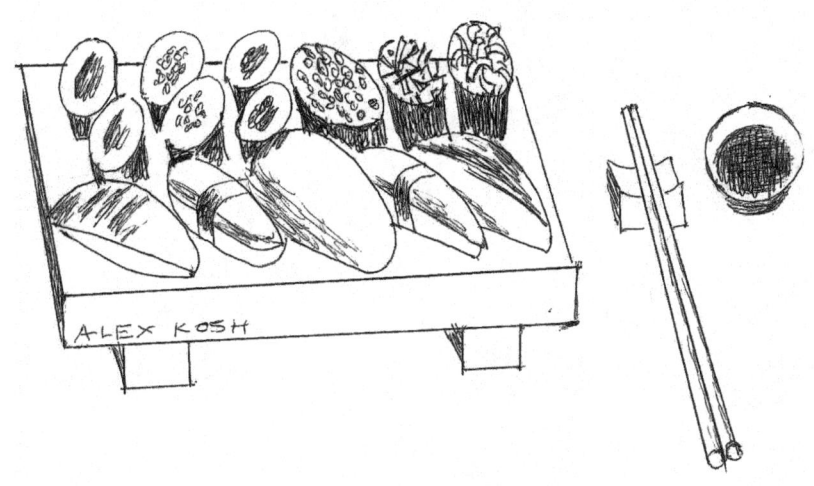

ALEX KOSH

Table Mementoes. Give them more time.

We spend this summer in Prealps. The house is in the middle of nowhere. One village ends half a mile down the hill from our house, and you need to walk at least fifteen minutes up the hill to the next one. No neighbours in sight, just hills, fields, dear and falcons. Everyone who visits us says that it is a paradise. I think they prefer to remain blind to the mole hills and insects. And my new peonies did not do particularly well this year. "Give them more time," my partner says. "They will blossom eventually." But I agree—it is clearly a paradise, at least for cucumbers.

We fell victim to the fad of raised garden beds. Courgettes, salad and slugs seemed a combination impossible, so we ended up with cucumbers. Who knew that cucumbers could be so aggressive? Whether it was us buying two too many (we bought three plants), or it was the horse manure we were advised to use by locals, everyone uses it they said and we believed. It smelt like that. Anyway, it doesn't matter. The result is that it is late July and cucumbers are omnipresent. All over the raised bed, on the lawn, on the terrace. On our table. I tried to pick them up when they were small. But I was outnumbered and they knew how to hide.

The web ran out of recipes. There is only that much you can make of a cucumber to satisfy your pallet I surrendered to cucumber and coconut salads, to pasta with onions, cucumbers and herbs, to asparagus and, guess what?, cucumber vinaigrette, to pineapple with basil (and cucumber), cucumber cups with French soups and cucumber-feta toasts... I actually developed some acquired taste for cucumber-and-lemon gin, but my partner being a rather observant man said that if it went like this any further, the empty gin bottles in the cellar would soon outstrip cucumbers in the garden.

Of course, when that invitation came, I was more than ready to go. Any dinner outside the cucumbers' nirvana at this point sounded like a bliss. And they live in the city! No raised garden beds there, I reckon.

"Who are they," I ask in the car.

"Some friends of Toby," says my partner. "Highflyers. He met them when he worked for that DIY shop. You remember, creating the empire for them all over the country—small towns big ideas? We went together for dinner a few times when they would come to the city."

"And what are they doing in the city?"

"Ambitious people. Finally got it working, proper incomes, moved to civilisation. What are they doing? Enjoying life for the first time, Toby says. Generous, nice. Invite friends regularly. Happy to share their good fortune."

We stop at the flower shop. The one I like. Nothing special, no orchids or other fancy hotel plants. But they can make the most sophisticated bouquets in the world from something rustic and wild. Their flowers are from the meadows nearby rather than from a refrigerated lorry.

We arrive just in time. It is a block of flats, not far from the centre. It has an inquisitive concierge and some pictures on the walls next to the lift. We are given a passcode to the lift. We go to the last floor. It is a penthouse we are invited to, after all. The lift's doors open into the flat directly. It is a big open space with a balcony at the end of it. Amazing views over the city. I still like concrete jungles more than cucumber ones.

The room is full with a nice buzzing crowd. Toby is here

too. The hosts though are not to be seen. "They check the dining room," Toby laughs. "Control freaks with the manual to follow."

I am introduced to Helen and Andy few minutes later. They are really nice and very open. Andy is happy to talk about the way things went the last few years. And he has all the right to be proud. Things went really well indeed, not for him only. For his whole little company and his bunch of devoted co-workers too.

I am given another cocktail in a fresh glass. But it is not a free floating cucumber which grabs my attention. It is a sticker on the glass. A little bit washed out, but still pretty new. It sits rather close to the rim of the glass. Wouldn't feel nice on the lips. Doesn't add to the taste. And, I have to confess, I take labels off. Wherever they are. Even on underwear.

I need to get rid of it as soon as possible. It is not Helen's fault it still sits there – she has too many glasses to take care of. The most important thing is to get rid of it before others see that someone has been served a "branded" glass here.

I start scratching the label off. It is not as easy as it sounds as I have a hobby which doesn't allow me to grow long nails. I play keyboards. Nails hitting the keys don't add to music. My music teacher is very strict insisting on me cutting them short. The label doesn't budge but I persevere.

Suddenly I feel a warm gentle hand on my arm.

"Oh, no, love. Don't," says Helen. "Leave it there. People appreciate the drinks more if they know they drink it from the proper glassware. How otherwise would they know it is Riedel?"

Chapter 8. Table manners, self-esteem and mental health

Self-esteem, one of the top level human needs is very often drawn from being a valuable member of a group. People respect themselves more when they excel in norms and values shared by the group they belong to and get approval from the senior members of this group whether the seniority is derived from age or mastery. The easiest example would be the workplace ID. Many of us identify ourselves through our profession and/or education. We also respect ourselves for less obvious matters. For refraining from that piece of cake, for example. And, of course, for holding the cutlery properly. Remember the easy way to be a good boy?

Etiquette and table manners are social constructs. There is no point in social conventions if there are no other people around. You can even eat your baked beans out of the can over the kitchen sink. It is easier to clean afterwards. That what I thought last year. I was wrong. Eating over the kitchen sink is not a recluse experience anymore. A Portuguese student explained to me that it is actually a very social thing to do. According to him it is not only a perfectly acceptable behaviour when you are on your own, it is also a socially shared momentum and even a great bonding exercise. How many students can you get over the kitchen sink? I am happy I don't have to live at a hall of residence anymore.

If identification with and acceptance into desirable social group, be it class or colleagues, requires certain skills, our self-esteem growths when we reach certain standards. Table manners, required for any successful interaction around the table are no exclusion. This is a gut factor at work, much more serious and much more important than it might seem.

Compliance with socially desirable behaviour is so much embedded in our perception of ourselves, that we continue practising socially adequate behaviour whether we have a company or are on our own. Very few of us would eat abstaining from any cutlery even if no one has a chance to see us.

"Dinner for one" is a movie basically unknown in England, but it is seen as an epitome of things everything English in Germany and Austria. It is on TV every Christmas. This is the best example of apotheosis of self-esteem derived from table manners, both for the lonely lady and her getting-ever-more-drunk butler. There is no way I can describe it. Just watch it on YouTube[14]

Impostor syndrome is well known today. It is described as a phenomenon which "occurs among high achievers who are unable to internalize and accept their success. They often attribute their accomplishments to luck rather than to ability, and fear that others will eventually unmask them as a fraud." (Weir, 2013) People, suffering from Impostor syndrome do not question their individual decisions or are concerned with lack of skills or knowledge in particular area. They question whether they belong to the group they joined in general. They doubt trivialities they see as connected to the new status, they question every move and if new status involves new table manners, the abundance of cutlery can drive them mad. When you struggle with simple things, it makes you question your overall association with your new status. It doesn't help your self-esteem. And low self-esteem can lead to mental health problems. (Mind, 2013)

Inclusivity of table manners is not limited to feeling of socially belonging only. Table manners are a tell-tale side of our mental health. Of whether we are all there, or out of our minds. Table manners constitute an important part of mental recovery programmes. "Staff members also teach personal care skills and table manners at grooming and meal times, the logical environments to learn these skills. Developing those skills and manners is essential to one day fitting into the general population, Meditto says" (KERSTING, January 2005, Vol 36, No. 1). The recovery of table manners could be a sign of overall improvement in mental health. The consultant psychiatrist said that he could clearly see at meal times in the hospital who is on the road to recovery.

> *"You see someone taking cutlery and napkins, being careful on how they handle them. Sitting at the table with a napkin on the lap and using cutlery again, not the hands, to eat. You get this feeling - they want to join back the social life. And this is the easiest way to show: I am human. I belong to a group who eat like me."*

Chapter 9. Convergence and globalisation

One of the very interesting modern trends is convergence in many areas of our lives. Most of us are using Windows, both for business and for private lives; google is a verb, even if we use different search engines; there is only a finite amount of car makes and you can find your favourite soft drink, be it cola or red bull in the majority of countries you have to travel to on business. It is a pity that the small shops disappear from High Street, but having a variety of restaurants with cuisine from all over the world is a clear plus. You can protest about globalisation, but the chances are you will do it on Facebook.

The biggest secret of market research is that we are more similar than we like to admit. There is some variation, but it is still possible to categorise, do the cluster analysis and segmentation research in any country you need to. You have to adjust your measurement for cultural differences, for example, Italians are known for being much more enthusiastic than their Northern counterparts. But – we all have more in common than we like to admit sometimes. If we really would be as individual as we like to think we are, then the long list of things would not be possible: statistics, dialects, vaccines and medical treatments, the medicines all together, literature and high street fashion to name just a few.

Globalisation has two-fold consequences. It allows you to get to know the world better, bringing it to the shop around the corner, but it also makes the other corner shop, thousands of miles away, looking exactly like yours.

When it comes to table manners, they also change under the influence of globalisation. Eating pizza with fingers becomes

more acceptable in Britain, eating peas with a fork becomes wider spread in China. Globalisation is about the change in social pressures, change in identity formation process, change in mechanisms of social controls and change in our judgements on what is "in" and what is "out."

When it comes to table manners in big corporations, it is already happening to some extent. How you eat at social outings is less determined by your "lesser," family ID, but more by peers. If they all eat "zig-zag" style only, it is easier to accept it simply because judgement in global business is based on business hierarchy, not directly on your social ID, class, table manners or upbringing in general. Judgement is based on how useful you are to your business. If your table manners are not really barbaric, if you don't present an immediate danger at the table to everyone's health and well-being, and if you haven't been suspected couple of times of trying to kill your competition with your cutlery, there are always some etiquette courses out there if you don't know which glass is for what. But business acumen is more difficult and more expensive to teach.

Although there is a real potential for some homogenisation of table manners helped by popular food related TV shows and democratisation of travel, there will be always some room for secret rituals and aspirational developments. There is another thing which makes me believe that globalisation of table manners is not something really likely. Smaller entertainment budgets and containment measures as the result of recent financial crises resulted in home-made sandwiches at your own desk becoming the most popular option for working lunch. With communication being immediate and huge screens selling for peanuts, we all can indulge in virtual sharing of our lunch. It has a huge advantage. One can always switch the camera off if unsure of his table manners.

Chapter 10. The paradox of etiquette

Etiquette is impossible without judgement. We have to spell it out: this is good. This is bad. Otherwise what do you teach? Which manners? The role of judgement is reflected in our language: "Don't eat as a pig," "We don't do it here." "Do you want to be like Mr X? Nobody will give you a hand." We judge people. It is one of social control mechanisms. When there is no judgement – everything goes. And who knows where it could lead.

> *"I am not one to judge, you know I am not one to judge. But that house is full of fat children"* (Lewis, 2013)

Judgement is behind our longing to learn better manners, to become more civilised. Judgement is behind the selling power of fear. "How to be a lady" type of books would never ever sell in today's world if not-being lady-like would not be looked down on. We don't want to be left out by unintentional faux-pas, that's why we learn the rules. We want to be judged positively. We want to belong, to be let in and to be "kept in" in the social groups we want to be identified with, even if publicly we claim to be an individual and against social pressures. We do it only because those claims allow us to feel belonging to the group we aspire to – the group of renowned nonconformists.

Etiquette teachers practise a lot of negative judgement criticising manners, habits, quality of service, etc. Otherwise what do you sell if there is nothing to improve?

At the same time etiquette requires to show no judgement whatsoever. No rolled eyes, no condescending, no patronising and no disdain. At least not in public. Is it hypocrisy or is it an effective social mechanism ensuring safety and pleasantry of daily dealings between humans, enhancing our sense of belonging and love, boosting our self-esteem and bringing in efficiency and success in our communication with "others"?

The main purpose of etiquette is twofold: to make others feel good in our company and to ensure that our interactions with others are smooth and successful. The main principle of etiquette is respect to others. That's what the rules are based upon. But the learning starts with someone telling you what is good and in, and what is out.

My mother fully agrees with me that there are no universally good and unarguably bad table manners. "You are right," she says. "There are manners and there is lack of them."

Works Cited

Catherine Saint Louis . (2013, August 9). *Rituals Make Our Food More Flavorful.* Retrieved from The New YorkTimes Blogs: http://well.blogs.nytimes.com/2013/08/09/rituals-make-our-food-more-flavorful

Adams, D. (1997). *The Hitchhiker's Guide to the Galaxy.* Del Rey Books.

Akkoc, R. (2014, November 18). *Beer sales around the world - who drinks the most?* Retrieved from Telegraph: http://www.telegraph.co.uk/finance/newsbysector/retailandconsumer/leisure/11237013/Mapped-Beer-sales-around-the-world-who-drinks-the-most.html

Albert Mehrabian, M. W. (1967). Decoding of Inconsisten Communications. *Journal of Personalityand Social Psychology 6 (1)*, 109-114.

Alexander, N. (2014). *The Half LIfe of Hanna.* Kindle Edition: BIGfib Books.

Ann Barr and Peter York. (1983). *The official Sloane Ranger Diary.* London: Ebury Press.

Arthur Inch and Arlene Hirst. (2003). *Dinner is served. A Butler's Guide to the art of the Table.* London-Philadelphia: Running Press Book Publishers.

Baer, D. (2015, April 28). *The scientific reason why Barack Obama and Mark Zuckerberg wear the same outfit every day.* Retrieved from Business Insider: http://www.businessinsider.com/barack-obama-mark-zuckerberg-wear-the-same-outfit-2015-4?IR=T

BBC News. (2016, March 11). *Thousands warned not to use 'high chlorine' water.* Retrieved from BBC : http://

www.bbc.com/news/uk-england-derbyshire-35786378

Bodleian Library. (2013). *How to dine in Style. The art of entertaining, 1920.* Oxford: University of Oxford.

Borreli, L. (2016, March 15). *The Power Of The Mind: Use Your Imagination To Curb Food Cravings.* Retrieved from Medical Daily Pulse: http://www.medicaldaily.com/appetite-suppressant-food-cravings-mind-trick-377917?rel=most_read5

Boscamp, E. (2013, July 11). *Dining etiquette from around the world.* Retrieved from Huffington Post: http://www.huffingtonpost.com/2013/07/11/dining-etiquette-around-the-world_n_3567015.html

Boundless. (2016, March 19). *Informal Means of Control.* Retrieved from www.boundless.com: https://www.boundless.com/sociology/textbooks/boundless-sociology-textbook/deviance-social-control-and-crime-7/social-control-60/informal-means-of-control-369-3188/

Carpenter, D. S. (September 2012). That gut feeling. *American Psychological Association Vol 43, No. 8,* 50.

Chopra, D. (2016, March 23). Retrieved from Brainy Quote: http://www.brainyquote.com/quotes/keywords/anticipation.html

Clayton, N. (2007). *A Butler's Guide to Table Manners.* National Trust Books.

Cleveland Clinic . (2016, March). *Eat well. Seasonal eating.* Retrieved from Cleveland Clinic Welness: http://www.clevelandclinicwellness.com/food/SeasonalEating/Pages/introduction.aspx

Cohen, J. (2012, June 12). *10 Worst Germ Hot Spots.* Retrieved from Forbes: http://www.forbes.com/sites/jennifercohen/2012/06/12/10-worst-germ-hot-spots/#49f5afa178ce

Conlin, J. (2014, June 20). *Translating English Protocol for a Wider Audience. Mind your manners, English style.* Retrieved from The New York Times: http://www.nytimes.com/2014/06/22/fashion/mind-your-manners-english-style.html

Cooper, J. (1999). *Class.* London: Corgi Books, Transworld Publishers.

Curry, R. (1996). *Too Much Of A Good Thing: Mae West as Cultural Icon.* Univ Of Minnesota Press.

Dalai Lama XIV. (2016, March 16). *quotes about rules.* Retrieved from goodReads: http://www.goodreads.com/quotes/tag/rules

Daly, J. (2014, December 8). *John Daly: What is etiquette and where did it originate from?* Retrieved from Nooshawk.com: It shouldn't surprise you that the French started it all! Today's etiquette began in the French royal courts in the 1600s and 1700s. Etiquette used to mean "keep off the grass."

Dean, C. T. (2015, February 26). *Pictured: The moment couple who ran away from a restaurant without paying $230 bill return to hand over the money after being shamed in social media campaign* . Retrieved from Daily Mail: http://www.dailymail.co.uk/news/article-2970311/Pictured-moment-couple-ran-away-restaurant-without-paying-230-bill-return-hand-money-shamed-social-media-campaign.html

Drachenfels, S. v. (2000). *The art of the table. A complete Guide to table setting, table manners, and tableware.* USA: Simon & Schuster.

Duignan, B. (2015, May 22). *Epicureanism.* Retrieved from Encyclopaedia Britannica, Inc.: http://www.britannica.com/topic/Epicureanism

Edwardes, C. (2014, January 22). *Report: The world's top*

prostitutes. Retrieved from Tatler: http://www.tatler.com/ news/articles/january-2014/the-worlds-top-prostitutes

Everett, F. (2011, March 3). *How I learned to be a princess! Kate Middleton is said to be taking lessons in royal etiquette... so what will she be learning?* Retrieved from Daily Mail: http://www.dailymail.co.uk/femail/article-1362394/Kate-Middleton-said-taking-royal-etiquette-lessons-princess.html

Flora, C. (2007, May 1). *Gut almighty.* Retrieved from Psychology today: https://www.psychologytoday.com/ articles/200705/gut-almighty

Food Standards Agency. (2016, March 20). *Allergy and intolerance: guidance for businesses.* Retrieved from Food Standards Agency: /www.food.gov.uk/sites/default/files/food-allergen-labelling-technical-guidance.pdf

Fox, K. (2004). *Watching the English.* GB: Hodder & Stoughton.

Fox, K. (2016). *Passport to the Pub.* Retrieved from SIRC Social Issues Research Centre: http://www.sirc.org/publik/ pub.html

Freedman, E. F. (2016, March 23). *Your Fork Is Not a Shovel: Business Etiquette and Know-How for Today's New Professional.* Retrieved from Employment Crossing: http:// www.employmentcrossing.com/article/230253/Your-Fork-Is-Not-a-Shovel-Business-Etiquette-and-Know-How-for-Today-s-New-Professional/

Furness, H. (2012, November 22). *How to eat with one's fingers: the Debrett's guide to very modern etiquette.* Retrieved from The Telegraph: http://www.telegraph.co.uk/ foodanddrink/foodanddrinknews/9696223/How-to-eat-with-ones-fingers-the-Debretts-guide-to-very-modern-etiquette.html

Gigerenzer, G. (2007). *Gut feelings. The intelligence of the unconsious.* USA: Viking Penguin .

Goodrich, H. (2013, March 18). *10 reasons why we should eat insects.* Retrieved from The Telegraph: http://www.telegraph.co.uk/culture/tvandradio/9937633/10-reasons-why-we-should-eat-insects.html

Gruenwald, K. (2016, March 13). *10 Eating Habits of The Queen Revealed by Royal Chef.* Retrieved from RecipesPlus: http://recipes-plus.com/article/10-eating-habits-queen-revealed-royal-chef-53

Gumpoltsberger, G. (2015, October 9). *EU-Food Information to Consumers Regulation.* Retrieved from WKO: https://www.wko.at/Content.Node/branchen/oe/Gastronomie/Lobbying---Branchenthemen/Allergeninfos-English.html

Highgate Mums. (2015). Retrieved from Facebook: www.facebook.com/HighgateMums

IMDb users. (2010-2016). *Quotes for Violet Crawley.* Retrieved from IMDb: http://www.imdb.com/character/ch0249425/quotes

Kanalley, C. (2011, August 2). *Donald Trump Explains Why He Eats His Pizza With A Fork.* Retrieved from Huffington Politics: http://www.huffingtonpost.com/2011/06/02/donald-trump-pizza-video_n_870519.html

Kathleen D. Vohs, Y. W. (2013, January 15). *Rituals Enhance Consumption.* Retrieved from Psychological Science. A Journal of the Association for Psychological Science.: http://pss.sagepub.com/content/24/9/1714

KERSTING, K. (January 2005, Vol 36, No. 1). Serious Rehabilitation. *Monitor on Psychology*, 38.

Lambert, C. (2007, January-February). *The Science of*

Happiness. Retrieved from Harvard Magazine: http://harvardmagazine.com/2007/01/the-science-of-happiness.html

Lewis, L. (2013, October 7). *24 Things Uttered By Highgate Mums.* Retrieved from BuzzFeed: http://www.buzzfeed.com/lukelewis/things-said-by-highgate-mums

Li, D. K. (2015, April 7). *David Cameron caught eating hot dog with knife and fork.* Retrieved from New York Post: http://nypost.com/2015/04/07/david-cameron-caught-eating-hot-dog-with-knife-and-fork/

Martin, M. (2013, July 15). *Kings Over the Water: Jacobite glass in the National Gallery of Victoria.* Retrieved from National Gallery of Victoria: http://www.ngv.vic.gov.au/essay/kings-over-the-water-jacobite-glass-in-the-national-gallery-of-victoria/

McConnell, A. R. (2010, September 18). *Reflection criticalfor self-improvement.* Retrieved from Psychology today: www.psychologytoday.com/blog/the-social-self/201009/reflection-critical-self-improvement

Meshanko, P. (2013). *The Respect Effect: Using the Science of Neuroleadership to Inspire a More Loyal and Productive Workplace.* USA: McGraw-Hill Education.

Mind. (2013). *How to increase your self-esteem.* Retrieved from Mind. For better mental health.: http://www.mind.org.uk/information-support/types-of-mental-health-problems/self-esteem/consequences-of-low-self-esteem/

Moore, A. (2013, March 1). *Why Does My Dog... Bury Bones and Other Objects?* Retrieved from vetSTREET. Your pet. Your vet.: http://www.vetstreet.com/our-pet-experts/why-does-my-dog-bury-objects

Nauert, R. (2006, October 6). *Anxiety More Common in Women*. Retrieved from PsychCentral: http://psychcentral.com/news/2006/10/06/anxiety-more-common-in-women/312.html

Paula M. S. Romão, A. M. (Vol. 35, No. 3 (Aug., 1990)). Human Saliva as a Cleaniin Agent for Dirty Surfaces. *Studies in Conservation*, 153-155.

Peretti, J. (2014, July 6). *SUVs, handwash and FOMO: how the advertising industry embraced fear*. Retrieved from The Guardian: http://www.theguardian.com/media/2014/jul/06/how-advertising-industry-concept-fear

Pym, H. (2015, September 17). *Is this cuddly robot coming to a care home near you?* Retrieved from BBC.com Health section: http://www.bbc.com/news/health-34271927

Quoidbach et al., & Jordi Quoidbach, E. W. (2015). The Price of Abundance. How a Wealth of Experiences Impoverishes Savoring. *Pers Soc Psychol Bull; vol. 41, 3*, 393-404.

Quote. (2016, March 23). *Quote*. Retrieved from Quote.net: http://www.quotes.net/quote/35953

Raw Food Explained. (2016, March 16). *Emotional aspects of diet and digestion*. Retrieved from Raw food explained: http://www.rawfoodexplained.com/nutrition-mind-and-the-emotions/emotional-aspects-of-diet-and-digestion.html

Richey, L. T. (2015, December 3). *How to Teach Children Table Manners*. Retrieved from Manners ToGo: http://www.mannerstogo.com/blog/how-to-teach-your-children-table-manners

Robin Fox. (1999, March 31). *Food and Eating: An Anthropological Perspective*. Retrieved from SIRC Social Issues Research Centre: http://www.sirc.org/publik/

food_and_eating_3.html

Royal Holloway, University of London. (2013, November 7). *Study shows trustworthy people perceived to look similar to ourselves*. Retrieved from Science Daily: www.sciencedaily.com/releases/2013/11/131107094406.htm

Ruiz, M. (2015, November 12). *Can a Commoner Learn Kate Middleton Grace?* Retrieved from Vogue: http://www.vogue.com/13370546/kate-middleton-british-etiquette-class/

Saad, G. (2009, June 9). *The Triggers of Envy Are Different for Men and Women*. Retrieved from Psychology Today: https://www.psychologytoday.com/blog/homo-consumericus/200906/the-triggers-envy-are-different-men-and-women

SAMHSA. (2016, 03 2013). *Cultural competence*. Retrieved from SAMHSA: http://www.samhsa.gov/capt/applying-strategic-prevention/cultural-competence

Sanghani, R. (2014, April 7). *Why this man takes photos of 'Women Who Eat On Tubes'. He promises he isn't a 'weird deviant'*. Retrieved from Telegraph, UK: http://www.telegraph.co.uk/women/womens-life/10749681/Why-this-man-takes-photos-of-Women-Who-Eat-On-Tubes.-He-promises-he-isnt-a-weird-deviant.html

Schweitzer, S. M. (2005, September 22). *When Better is Worse: Envy and the Use of Deception in Negotiations*. Retrieved from SSRN Social Science Research Network: http://papers.ssrn.com/sol3/papers.cfm?abstract_id=804844

Shere, J. (2010, July 21). *Did You Know That Laughter Is Good For Your Health?* Retrieved from Indiana Public Media: http://indianapublicmedia.org/amomentofscience/laughter-good-for-health/

Showell, B. (2014, December 7). *We Tried It: An Etiquette Class Based on Princess Kate.* Retrieved from People: http://www.people.com/people/package/article/0,,20395222_20880298,00.html

Socrates. (2016, March 15). *Socrates Quotes.* Retrieved from goodReads: http://www.goodreads.com/quotes/63219-the-children-now-love-luxury-they-have-bad-manners-contempt

The Economist, Special Report. (2006, December 19). *The art of conversation. Chattering Classes.* Retrieved from The economist: http://www.economist.com/node/8345491

Vaillant, G. E. (2012). *Triumphs of Experience. The men of the Harvard Grant Study.* Cambridge, Massachusetts, London: The Belknap Press of Harvard University Press.

Vanessa Harrar and Charles Spence. (2013, June 26). *The taste of cutlery: how the taste of food is affected by the weight, size, shape, and colour of the cutlery used to eat it.* Retrieved from BioMed Central: http://flavourjournal.biomedcentral.com/articles/10.1186/2044-7248-2-21

Visser, M. (1992). *The Rituals of Dinner: The Origins, Evolution, Eccentricities and Meaning of Table Manners.* Penquin Books.

Weir, K. (2013, November). *Feeling like a Fraud?* Retrieved from American Psychological Association: http://www.apa.org/gradpsych/2013/11/fraud.aspx

Wendy Donahue, C. T. (2015, April 5). *Don't invite lawyers to your kid's birthday party.* Retrieved from PANTAGRAPH: http://www.pantagraph.com/lifestyles/don-t-invite-lawyers-to-your-kid-s-birthday-party/article_b3264bac-6c48-5c19-8f4c-45ce0f7660be.html

Wikipedia. (2016, March 13). *Cultural Competence.* Retrieved

from Wikipedia: http://en.wikipedia.org/wiki/
Cultural_competence

Wikipedia. (2016, March 14). *Maslow's hierarchy of needs*. Retrieved from Wikipedia, the free encyclopedia: https://en.wikipedia.org/wiki/Maslow's_hierarchy_of_needs

York, P. (2007). *Cooler, Faster, More Expensive. The Return of the Sloane Ranger*. London: Atlantic Books.

ENDNOTES:

[1] You can read more on how to pour different beer German style here: http://www.businessinsider.com/how-to-pour-beer-like-a-german-2015-8?IR=T

[2] Karl Marx is buried in Highgate Cemetery East. He moved to London in 1849 and died there in 1883.

[3] AI- artificial intelligence.

[4] You can read more how stress affects digestion here: http://www.everydayhealth.com/hs/better-digestion/how-stress-affects-digestion/ and http://psychologyofeating.com/4-ways-stress-impacts-digestion/

[5] BBC television drama series about secret services and spies. It was broadcast as MI-5 in some other countries, including the US.

[6] "A table of joy" is a method used for solving mathematical problems involving proportions : http://www.dummies.com/how-to/content/how-the-table-of-joy-works-for-basic-maths.html

[7] It is absolutely fine to use no table linen at all if the occasion is not strictly formal and your table is not exceptionally ugly.

[8] He refers to so-called "French service," when the waiter brings half-ready food to the table and finishes cooking in front of the guests.

[9] http://www.telegraph.co.uk/women/womens-life/10766093/Women-Who-Eat-on-Tubes-Meet-the-London-ladies-who-lunch-on-the-Tube.html

[10]Kyrgyzstan detains Briton for 'horse penis' delicacy comparison. The Guardian. 3/01/2016 http://www.theguardian.com/world/2016/jan/03/british-worker-kyrgyzstan-gold-mine-held-horse-penis-delicacy-comparison

[11] More details on this study http://www.artofmanliness.com/2014/09/02/love-is-all-you-need-insights-from-the-longest-longitudinal-study-on-men-ever-conducted/

[12] UK's broadsheet newspaper.

[13] More on social anomie could be found here: http://www.britannica.com/topic/anomie

[14] Dinner for One. Watch it here https://youtu.be/zVd_VLO9xcc and read about it here en.wikipedia.org/wiki/Dinner_for_One